Esther and Ruth

INTERPRETATION
BIBLE STUDIES

Esther and Ruth

PATRICIA K. TULL

Westminster John Knox Press
LOUISVILLE • LONDON

Book design by Drew Stevens
Cover design by Pam Poll
Cover illustration by Robert Stratton

First edition
Published by Westminster John Knox Press
Louisville, Kentucky

This book is printed on acid-free paper that meets the American National Standards Institute Z39.48 standard. ♾

PRINTED IN THE UNITED STATES OF AMERICA

03 04 05 06 07 08 09 10 11 12 — 10 9 8 7 6 5 4 3 2 1

Library of Congress Cataloging-in-Publication Data is on file at the Library of Congress, Washington, D.C.

ISBN 0-664-22670-1

Contents

Series Introduction

The Bible has long been revered for its witness to God's presence and redeeming activity in the world; its message of creation and judgment, love and forgiveness, grace and hope; its memorable characters and stories; its challenges to human life; and its power to shape faith. For generations people have found in the Bible inspiration and instruction, and, for nearly as long, commentators and scholars have assisted students of the Bible. This series, Interpretation Bible Studies (IBS), continues that great heritage of scholarship with a fresh approach to biblical study.

Designed for ease and flexibility of use for either personal or group study, IBS helps readers not only to learn about the history and theology of the Bible, understand the sometimes difficult language of biblical passages, and marvel at the biblical accounts of God's activity in human life, but also to accept the challenge of the Bible's call to discipleship. IBS offers sound guidance for deepening one's knowledge of the Bible and for faithful Christian living in today's world.

IBS was developed out of three primary convictions. First, the Bible is the church's scripture and stands in a unique place of authority in Christian understanding. Second, good scholarship helps readers understand the truths of the Bible and sharpens their perception of God speaking through the Bible. Third, deep knowledge of the Bible bears fruit in one's ethical and spiritual life.

Each IBS volume has ten brief units of key passages from a book of the Bible. By moving through these units, readers capture the sweep of the whole biblical book. Each unit includes study helps, such as maps, photos, definitions of key terms, questions for reflection, and suggestions for resources for further study. In the back of each volume is a Leader's Guide that offers helpful suggestions on how to use IBS.

The Interpretation Bible Studies series grows out of the well-known Interpretation commentaries (John Knox Press), a series that helps preachers and teachers in their preparation. Although each IBS volume bears a deep kinship to its companion Interpretation commentary, IBS can stand alone. The reader need not be familiar with the Interpretation commentary to benefit from IBS. However, those who want to discover even more about the Bible will benefit by consulting Interpretation commentaries too.

Through the kind of encounter with the Bible encouraged by the Interpretation Bible Studies, the church will continue to discover God speaking afresh in the scriptures.

Introduction to Esther and Ruth

A staggering 38 of the 66 books of the Protestant Bible are known by the names of men, either men who appear in them (such as Joshua or Job), men whose speeches are contained in them (such as Isaiah and other prophets), men to whom tradition attributes their authorship (such as the four Gospels), or men to whom they are addressed (such as Titus and Philemon). Only two books of the canon, Esther and Ruth, fourteen chapters total, bear women's names.

This disproportionate attention the Bible gives to men and male deeds may not have seemed strange to the ancient men who developed the biblical canon. But if modern people wonder what a lopsided view of human life has to offer contemporary communities of faith, their question is neither inappropriate nor too challenging to probe honestly.

Indeed, only a small percentage of the named characters in the Bible are women. Some of the most memorable women, such as the daughter of Jephthah (Judg. 11), the Levite's concubine (Judg. 19–21), the Syrophoenician woman (Mark 7), and the woman at the well (John 4), are presented namelessly. The Bible pulls no punches about the fates of women: They are raped (Dinah in Gen. 34, Tamar in 2 Sam. 13), forced into marriage (the dancers at Shiloh in Judg. 21, Esther in Esther 2), offered to other men by their fathers (Michal in 1 Sam. 18) or husbands (Sarah in Gen. 12 and 20), abandoned (Hagar in Gen. 16 and 21, Samson's wife in Judg. 14), dismembered (the Levite's concubine in Judg. 19), and murdered (Jezebel in 2 Kgs. 9, Athaliah in 2 Kgs. 11). They

---

List of Characters in Esther

Narrator
King Ahasuerus (chapters 1, 3, 5–9)
Esther (chapters 4, 5, 7–9)
Haman (chapters 3, 5–7)
Mordecai (chapter 4 only)
Memucan (chapter 1 only)
King's servants (chapters 2, 3, 6)
Zeresh and Haman's friends
  (chapters 5 and 6 only)
Harbona (chapter 7 only)

must fight for property (daughters of Zelophehad in Num. 27). They must prove their worth by bearing sons (Leah and Rachel in Gen. 29–30). They must survive by their wits (Tamar in Gen. 38, Shiphrah and Puah in Exod. 1, Jael in Judg. 4, Abigail in 1 Sam. 25, the wise women of 2 Sam. 14 and 20) and by their tenacity (Moses' mother in Exod. 2, Delilah in Judg. 16, Bathsheba in 1 Kgs. 1, the Shunammite woman in 2 Kgs. 4).

Yet if the biblical world is a fairly unsafe place for women, it mirrors the experience of most women still. Women's freedom even in the first world remains tenuous, constricted by the fear of attack by strangers, employers, and husbands. In many parts of the third world, women's freedom hardly exists at all. That is why stories of courageous women still stand out disproportionately to their length in the biblical canon—because we still need them so very much. Stories of biblical women whose efforts are met by divine cooperation and community affirmation inspire hope for contemporary women, hope that even if women's lives are constrained by what Carol Bechtel calls the possession of only "limited power" and therefore the necessity to "steer from the front of the canoe" (Bechtel, 11), in the end the effort to do so will pay off in the realization of a better world for both women and men.

The Uniqueness of Esther and Ruth

Esther and Ruth are unique in the biblical canon not only by virtue of their names and subject matter. They also stand out as freestanding narratives, springing from Judean history but independent of the primary biblical storyline. In a few short chapters, each introduces a setting and cast of characters, complicates the plot, then resolves it, developing in the course of events not only clear pictures of these women and men as memorable people, but a sense of the way the world works—a theology of providence, broadly speaking.

This theology of providence is woven into both books in quite subtle ways. Despite their presence in the biblical canon, neither book is primarily concerned with what A. B. Rhodes called

---

List of Characters in Ruth

Narrator
Naomi (chapters 1–3)
Ruth (chapters 1–3)
Boaz (chapters 2–4)
Orpah (chapter 1)
Women of Bethlehem (chapters 1, 4)
The reapers and the man in charge of them (chapter 2)
The other kinsman (chapter 4)
Witnesses at the gate (chapter 4)

"the mighty acts of God." In Ruth, God is credited with the first and last acts of grace, but otherwise remains behind the scenes. In Esther, God is not mentioned at all, and any inferences about divine action must remain inferences. Both books reflect a subtlety of divine presence that resembles much more closely life in our own world than the pyrotechnics of Mount Sinai.

Like the rest of the Protestant Old Testament, Esther and Ruth are also canonical for the Jewish community. In the Christian Bible, each book was inserted into the place that seemed appropriate historically. Because Ruth begins, "In the days when the judges ruled," it was placed between Judges and 1 Samuel, where it provides a corrective to the horrifying story of the Levite's concubine, as well as a counterpart to the peaceful story of Hannah and Elkanah. Because Esther begins, "This happened in the days of Ahasuerus," a Persian emperor, Esther was placed by Christians after Ezra and Nehemiah, which also concern the Persian era.

> The three-part canon of Jewish scripture includes the Torah (Genesis through Deuteronomy), Nevi'im, or Prophets (Joshua, Judges, 1–2 Samuel, 1–2 Kings, Isaiah, Jeremiah, Ezekiel, and the Twelve Minor Prophets), and Ketuvim, or Writings (Psalms, Job, Proverbs, the five Megilloth, Daniel, Ezra, Nehemiah, and 1–2 Chronicles).

These placements have suggested more strongly than they perhaps should that the stories be read as historical event, obscuring their richness as biblical parable.

Jewish tradition, however, placed these stories within the third section of the Jewish Bible, or Tanakh, which is called *Ketuvim,* or "Writings." This section includes the Psalms, wisdom literature, late books such as Daniel, Chronicles, and Ezra-Nehemiah, and five short books—called the Megilloth, or Scrolls—which are traditionally read on important Jewish holy days. Ruth is the first of these Megilloth, and is read during the Feast of Weeks, or Pentecost, which celebrates not only the giving of the law on Mount Sinai but also the grain harvest. Esther is the last of the Megilloth, and celebrates the festival of Purim, which is instituted at the close of Esther's narrative. Interestingly, Ruth, with its emphasis on the "woman of strength" (Ruth 3:11), follows immediately the description in Proverbs 31 of the "woman of strength." Esther, the Jewish woman surviving by her wits among the Gentiles, immediately precedes the book of Daniel, with its similar setting in the courts of Gentile emperors.

Both Ruth and Esther have been rightly called by Johanna W. H. van Wijk-Bos "women in alien lands." Ruth is a Gentile woman from Moab who makes her home in Bethlehem. Esther is an Israelite living in exile among the Gentiles of Persia. Both books therefore are deeply involved in themes of inclusion and exclusion, not only in terms of gender but also in terms of ethnicity. Yet the situations of these two women are very different, and as a result, the narrative style unfolds with very distinct tones and purposes.

The Megilloth are Ruth (read on Pentecost), Song of Songs (read on Passover), Ecclesiastes (read on the Feast of Tabernacles, or Sukkot), Lamentations (read on the Ninth of Av, the date of the temple's destruction), and Esther (read on Purim).

Esther's is a world of danger from powerful and prideful enemies. As underdogs in this alien world, battling the immediate threat of genocide, Esther and her cousin Mordecai must survive by cunning and grit. Esther's narrator spares no quarter in destroying the pretensions of Esther's enemies by means of high satire and ribald humor. If readers are tempted both to laugh and cry as Esther unfolds, they are following the author's lead. As Carol Bechtel says of the story's dark humor, "We not only laugh until we cry; we laugh so that we will not cry" (Bechtel, 26).

The dangers in Ruth's environment are very different. The only enemy in her story is God, who, according to Ruth's mother-in-law, Naomi, has left them destitute and empty. Humans are not contrasted by their role as friends or enemies, but rather by the extent to which they supersede the bounds of societal expectation, becoming conduits of *hesed,* or covenant loyalty, to the needy among them. In the end, not only the people but also the vision of the divine is redeemed in the course of Ruth's story. Correspondingly, the narrative of Ruth is less funny, less angular, more pensive and gentle. In this study I have chosen, against conventional practice, to place Ruth last, not because it is a better story—each has its place—but because its harmonious picture of human community, while unfortunately seldom realized this side of the garden of Eden, leaves a more hopeful vision.

Suggestions for Beginning Study

Readers gathering to study Esther and Ruth for the first time would be well served to read through each book out loud as a group. Such a reading, which even for Esther takes less than an hour, allows participants to savor the suspenseful plots with all their twists and turns, before delving into the individual features of each story. Readers will enjoy the rich repetitions of plot elements, the foreshadowings and backward glances, and the insistent unfolding of ironic "coincidence" as each plot moves to complexity and resolution.

Like most of the Bible's narratives, Esther and Ruth lend themselves well to a "reader's theatre" approach. The leader may read the narrator's parts, with others joining in the speaking parts. (See pp. 1–2 for a list of major characters in each book.)

Whenever readers immerse themselves in a biblical text, connections emerge between the Bible and contemporary life in unexpected ways. When teaching the book of Esther extensively for the Presbyterian Church (U.S.A.) a few years ago, I coined the phrase, "having an Esther moment," for the many times themes from the book seemed to rise up and envelope a moment of personal or community life. During that study, many women told me stories of their own lives, of moments when the world changed for them, when they were called upon to grow up in ways they hadn't needed to before, to dig down deep to find courage to speak up on their own behalf or on behalf of others who were even more vulnerable than they—"Esther moments" in their own lives. Similarly, in the writing of this study, the story of Ruth, with its themes of community and providence, began to take shape in my own reflections and sermons.

 Want to Know More?

About leading Bible study groups? See Roberta Hestenes, *Using the Bible in Groups* (Philadelphia: Westminster Press, 1983); Christine Blair, *The Art of Teaching the Bible* (Louisville, Ky.: Geneva Press, 2001).

About symbols in the Old Testament? See Paul J. Achtemeier, ed., *HarperCollins Bible Dictionary*, rev. ed. (New York: Harper-Collins, 1996), 1076–79.

About divine providence in Ruth? See Katherine Doob Sakenfeld, *Ruth*, Interpretation (Louisville, Ky.: John Knox Press, 1999), 14–16.

About divine providence in Esther? See Carol Bechtel, *Esther*, Interpretation (Louisville, Ky.: John Knox Press, 2002), 10–14.

Throughout this study guide, suggestions are made for considering the connections between these ancient stories and our own stories. The most meaningful connections are made, however, in the imaginations and witness of readers themselves. May God bless the reading and hearing of these words!

Esther 1:1–2:4

Parties, Politics, and Power

Esther is one of several biblical books that, while canonical for Christians, is much better known by Jewish readers. The annual Jewish celebration of Purim centers upon a lively audience-participation reading of Esther, assuring that the book is well known and thoroughly enjoyed.

By contrast, Christians, especially white Christians, do not know Esther well. The book appears only once in the Revised Common Lectionary. Many introductions to the Old Testament omit or seriously abbreviate reference to Esther. Even some feminist scholars have expressed ambivalence toward Esther's less than outspoken personality. Yet the book's incisive explorations of violence and vengeance, of power and its abuse, and of racial and gender domination catch modern readers by surprise. It is well worth a new reading by Christians compelled by the connections between the biblical world and our own.

The story takes place in Susa, the capital city of the Persian Empire, during the reign of King Ahasuerus (Xerxes in Greek tradition) in the early fifth century B.C.E. Esther and her older cousin Mordecai are Jews living in Persia as a result of the Babylonian exile a century before. While Ahasuerus is a historical figure, and some of the customs cited reflect knowledge of Persian courts, several factual inconsistencies identify the

> "We should be careful not to equate fiction with untruth. To understand this, one only has to think of how truth manifests itself in any great work of fiction. Charles Dickens tells a great deal of truth, for instance, in his classic story *A Christmas Carol.* While many of its details are historically accurate, the story never sets out to be a chronicle of nineteenth-century England. Fiction, then, is not the absence of truth, but often the vehicle for it. Historical fiction, while drawing on both the outlines and details of history, is still intended to tell a truth that goes beyond historical accuracy." Bechtel, *Esther,* 4.

story as historical fiction rather than history. Foremost of these is that during the time that this story identifies the queen of Persia first as Vashti and then as Esther the Jew, both Persian and Greek records show that the king was actually required to marry from one of seven Persian families. Ahasuerus's queen throughout his reign was named Amestris, a woman about whom several unsavory facts are known.

The book's first line sets King Ahasuerus in the misty past from the standpoint of the author and readers. Most commentators believe the book to have been written between 400 and 200 B.C.E. As will be discussed in later chapters, the story of Esther has been transmitted to us in three very different versions, only one of which is familiar to most Jews and Protestants. A striking feature of these three versions is the difference among their theological perspectives. The version that is canonical for Jews and Protestants is the only one in which God never appears. This omission has raised religious eyebrows for millennia, and continues to do so today.

Who Are the Good Guys?

Contemporary readers of Esther often encounter difficulty discerning the narrator's sympathies as the story begins. When reading Gospel narratives, we are accustomed to identifying with Jesus as hero, and to sorting out our sympathies according to other characters' responses to him. In Old Testament stories, where heroes are usually presented as complex, morally ambiguous (or rather, poignantly finite) personalities, we gain clues by listening for the voice of God or of God's reliable spokespeople.

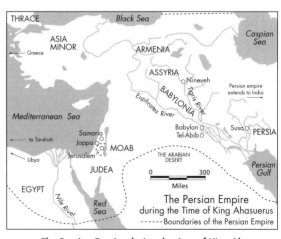

The Persian Empire during the time of King Ahasuerus

The first chapter of Esther, however, lacks overt signals directing our sympathies. Of course, Jesus does not appear. As was mentioned already, neither does God. Even more strikingly, no Israelites or Jews appear in the opening scenes. Readers are placed in a land foreign both to Israel and to ourselves, in the royal

7

court of an imperial ruler. The first episode confronts us with a Persian domestic crisis erupting into a national emergency. We must read carefully between the lines to discover the narrator's sympathies.

The Spendor and Pomp of His Majesty: Esther 1:1–9

The story opens with two sentences setting the events, as it were, long ago and far away, and yet suggesting that readers should recognize immediately the personage in command: "This happened in the days of Ahasuerus, the same Ahasuerus who ruled over one hundred twenty-seven provinces from India to Ethiopia. In those days when King Ahasuerus sat on his royal throne in the citadel of Susa, in the third year of his reign, he gave a banquet for all his officials and ministers" (1:1–3a).

Contemporary readers unfamiliar with such settings naturally miss many of the subtle exaggerations of the king's grandeur. As Bechtel notes, 127 provinces is about a hundred more than historians give the kings of Persia credit for. Such a clear exaggeration would have signaled to earliest readers that the story was opening not with factual reportage but with a hyperinflated account of royal pomp.

Details in the next several verses continue to inflate the royal privilege of King Ahasuerus. In the first two sentences the king's name is invoked three times, and regal descriptives abound: The words "ruled," "king," "royal," and "reign" all derive from the same Hebrew root and therefore present themselves, especially in the original language, as excessively repetitive. One punch line occurs at the end of verse 4, which describes exactly what the king was displaying to the officials, ministers, armies, nobles, and governors gathered in Susa: "the great wealth of his kingdom and the splendor and pomp of his majesty for many days." How many days? Not just five, ten, or thirty, but 180 days; that is, six whole months. By this point, careful readers may be wondering what the narrator is up to.

The next several verses linger in great detail over the physical descriptions of the king's banqueting hall—the actual ingredients, apparently, of the "splendor and pomp of his majesty." Carol Bechtel notes the danger of reading these descriptions too much from a first-world perspective. Typical Jewish readers in the Persian empire and for many centuries thereafter would have viewed the lavishness of the royal court not only as completely foreign to their own more frugal experience but even as morally suspect. But many American church-goers today inhabit, or aspire to inhabit, settings rivaling the king's in luxury if not in renown. Therefore, we can easily miss the irony as the narrator spins out descriptions worthy of home decorating magazines.

Sharp distinctions between the lavish description of Ahasuerus's two parties and the pointed lack of description accompanying the announcement of Queen Vashti's party may also be lost on readers who take for granted men's greater capacity for accumulating and spending wealth. The queen's party is barely mentioned at all, and then only as an aside after eight verses of description of the king's celebrations. We might suspect that the queen's banquet is left undescribed simply because it either mirrors the splendor of the king's festivities, and therefore doesn't justify the repetition, or lacks it, and therefore isn't worth describing. We must take care therefore, or we may find ourselves falling right into the gender assumptions the narrator is about to explode.

> "Jews and Protestants share a version of the book that is based on the Masoretic Text (MT), a Hebrew version that has been passed down by the rabbis and is regarded as canonical by both faith communities. Eastern Orthodox and Roman Catholic Christians, on the other hand, include a different version of Esther in their canons. It is based on the Greek Septuagint, a translation of a Hebrew original that differs from the MT in some respects. Most of these differences are relatively minor. There is, however, one major discrepancy where the book of Esther is concerned: The Septuagint includes six passages that are not in the MT." Bechtel, *Esther*, 1–2.

The Refusal of the Queen: Esther 1:10–22

What we may begin to recognize as gentle mocking of the excesses of foreign rulers turns serious very quickly when, on the final day of the king's second feast, he orders a procession of seven eunuchs to fetch his beautiful queen, the greatest of his possessions. One can almost see the inflated grandeur crushed as these servants trot out to bring her, and trot back in to announce her party-pooping refusal. Neither the king nor the readers are told why Vashti refuses this invitation. Given the length of the descriptions of the palace, some few words of explanation might have been expected. Yet words about Vashti's refusal are as terse as descriptions of her party.

Literary critics note that such information gaps draw readers in by inviting us to "connect the dots" with our own hypotheses, which often reflect our own experience-conditioned views. Did Vashti refuse out of impudence? Modesty? Anger? Was she ill, busy, apologetic, or incensed? Did she have any idea what the consequences might be? Commentators through the ages have speculated about Vashti. For instance, ancient rabbis said she was justly offended because the king was commanding her to appear before the men wearing *nothing but* her royal crown.

Readers are not the only spectators drawn into the evaluative fray. The furious king turns what could have been a private embarrassment into an imperial conflagration by calling in seven more men, seven sages, some of whose names strangely echo those of the seven eunuchs and are thus reduced narratively to yet another handful of henchmen.

Memucan's lengthy rhetoric is worth savoring. In the opinion of this spin doctor, Vashti's refusal is nothing short of a national emergency. If she is not punished severely, every woman in Persia will be out of control. Combining brazen flattery, flagrant gender profiling, and the most foolish solutions possible, Memucan suggests that the queen be banned from the very place she didn't want to be (that will show her!). Further, since it would be contrary to the king's interests for word of this debacle to spread, Memucan recommends sending a royal edict to all corners of the empire declaring what has happened. We are told that this advice pleases the king, and the royal implementation of this plan is detailed. An edict is sent out legislating morality in every household in Persia.

By this point, though we cannot hear the narrator's tone of voice, most readers have gathered that what is happening in Esther is not life in the real world, not even the world of ancient Persia. A master of irony, an ancient political cartoonist, the storyteller keeps a straight face, refrains from shrill editorials about government spending, moral turpitude, conspicuous consumption, and patriarchal pushiness, and disingenuously exposes the underside of imperial domination. When we add up the details, we realize that in the world of the Bible, the great foreign rulers are not quite as wholesome and good as our own leaders claim to be.

The Roundup of the Contestants: Esther 2:1–4

After Vashti is banished, the king needs a new queen. The king's advisors once again supply a flattering and overblown solution: The king ought to send out commissioners to every province to seek all the beautiful young virgins in the land and gather them to the king's palace. Not just some of these beauties, but all of them. There they will be prepared with cosmetic treatments for a whole year, and be brought one by one, night after night, to the king's chambers. One of them he will choose as queen, and all the rest will fill his harem. That is how Esther will soon enter the story: as one of the many, many beautiful young virgins who are conscripted for the king and made to go live in his palace.

As Bechtel notes, analogies to modern beauty pageants, though tempting, are quite misleading, since admission is involuntary and the king controls the losers as well as the winner. A closer contemporary analogy is the kidnapping of girls and women, lured into sexual slavery in foreign countries by false promises of respectable employment. On the one hand, readers might chuckle as the colossal imperial machinery gears up once again to mollify the whims of a world ruler who is slave both to his passions and to his advisors. On the other hand, the spectacle conveying the buffoonery of raw power is also horrifying. Nazi euphemisms such as "transfer" and "selection" are closer to the mark than "pageant" or "contest."

A double handful of motifs has been established in the story's opening that will carry throughout the book. One major recurring theme will be the banquets (literally, "drinking parties")—with interesting variations in the occasion and guest list—three of which have already transpired within the first nine verses. Outlandish royal laws and far-flung edicts sent out by an ancient form of pony express, most of these suggested by advisors to the king, will also dominate the book as they have dominated the opening scenes. Excessive and violent solutions to public relations snafus will reappear. Eunuchs will continue to serve

> The Hebrew word customarily translated as "banquet" or "feast" is *mishteh*, which derives from the verb "to drink." More properly translated, it is a drinking party.

as messengers and minions, and sycophants will continue their flattering rhetoric. Appearing before the king will become an issue for the new queen as well, a queen whose feelings and responses are, like Vashti's, kept private, veiled in modesty befitting a Persian princess. By contrast, the deeds, motives, and feelings of the king and his henchmen are exposed for the reader's critical scrutiny.

It is an entertaining story so far—funny, ironic, even infuriating. But what can we make of it theologically? The beginning of Esther teaches us nothing directly about God. It does, however, broaden our views of scripture and of scripture's concerns and modes of speaking. Frivolous abuse of power is funny only to those not suffering its effects. What the author of Esther attacks by means of satire and hyperbole, Hebrew prophets such as Amos and Isaiah vigorously condemned, the Psalms and Lamentations grieved, and the Gospel writers exposed by pointed contrast with Jesus' words and deeds. Throughout scripture, in the words of the Magnificat, God is portrayed as casting down the powerful from their thrones and lifting up the lowly (Luke 1:52). The opening of Esther prepares the way for such a storyline.

Want to Know More?

About the Babylonian exile? See Paul J. Achtemeier, ed., *HarperCollins Bible Dictionary*, rev. ed. (New York: HarperCollins, 1996), 97–99.

About issues of historicity in Esther? See Moore, *Esther*, xxxiv–xlvi; and Bechtel, *Esther*, 2–4.

About literary criticism of the Bible? See Adele Berlin, *Poetics and Interpretation of Biblical Narrative* (Sheffield: Almond Press, 1983); Robert Alter, *The Art of Biblical Narrative* (New York: Basic Books, 1981).

More specifically, the events at the beginning of Esther sharply elucidate the constricted world of women not only in ancient Persia but in many parts of contemporary society. Vashti had no acceptable choices. We may admire her independence, but we must also acknowledge the trouble her clash with authority occasioned for her and other women. For the author to chronicle her story is in itself an act of defiance against the fate of many women who have no real choices in their societies. While the Bible is notoriously scanty in its attention to women's lives, the portrayals that do occur are often both incisive and heartbreaking, reflecting a God who never intended such conditions as Vashti and the other brides endure in this story.

? Questions for Reflection

1. The author writes that the book of Esther is more popular in Jewish tradition than Christian. Have you read or studied the book of Esther before? If so, in what setting?
2. What do you read into Vashti's refusal to appear before the king, as he commanded? Why was the reaction of the king and his henchmen so overblown?
3. In her Interpretation commentary, Carol Bechtel notes that comparing the king's search for a new queen to a modern-day beauty pageant is misleading. To what modern-day events would you compare this search?
4. What does the story so far say about the status of women in ancient Persia?

Personnel, Programs—and Pogroms

As we saw in the previous chapter, the great machinery of the Persian imperial system churns for the pleasure of its ruler. Extravagant and lengthy drinking parties in luxury-laden settings emphasize his opulence and benevolence. Groups of royal henchmen—eunuchs, advisors, and servants—rush to ensure his happiness, while both the legal system and the postal system serve his direct benefit.

The one flaw in all the empire seems to be the need to force women to get with the royal program. While the benefits of seeking the king's pleasure have so far been taken for granted by the men, women seem to need guidance understanding their place. The one woman most expected to set an example of queenly pliability simply refused to play the game. Recognizing her act as powerful and potentially influential, royal officials have twice legislated worldwide womanly compliance: first, by ordering all married women to obey their husbands, and second, by rounding up the unmarried for the king's pleasure. Though the narration keeps a light touch, we should not forget the disruption and even violence implied in such actions. All is not right in the world of King Ahasuerus.

The cracks in the facade of Susa will only widen. Chapter 2 introduces us to Esther and Mordecai, two Jewish exiles, and establishes their place in the royal court. Chapter 3 introduces us to Haman, an arch-villain if there ever was one.

A Jew in the Royal Harem: Esther 2:5–23

Much of biblical literature reflects ambivalent, if not negative, relations between Jews and foreign rulers. Though raised in Pharaoh's court,

Moses rebelled and led the Hebrews from Egypt. In the days of the judges and kings, neighbors such as the Philistines, Moabites, Ammonites, Syrians, Egyptians, and Assyrians tried in vain to subjugate Israel. Court stories such as the tales of Daniel demonstrate resistance to assimilation. So when a forcible conscription of damsels occurs, separating a Jewish woman from her kin, we may expect a story of resistance at least as forceful as Vashti's, and much more successful. What transpires instead, namely, the young Esther's cooperation and even success in the royal harem, may cause readers to wonder where this story is going: Will Vashti the Gentile be a better Jew than the actual Jew Esther? Or will this story, over against the biblical norm, advocate the tactical advantages of compliance and even assimilation?

Esther presented to Ahasuerus

The evidence unfolds ambiguously in chapter 2. Mordecai is presented along with an explanation of his lineage and his presence in Persia, with heavy emphasis on his status as exile. Esther's presentation stresses her vulnerability even more: She is young, beautiful, Jewish, and orphaned. She hides both her real name and her kindred. The first several verbs surrounding her show her being acted upon: She was brought up, adopted, taken, and put. However, unlike Vashti, both Esther and Mordecai not only comply with the king's self-serving law, but energetically seek to work their way into his favor.

Esther's appeal seems almost magical. She wins the favor of the eunuch Hegai and is given special treatment (v. 9). She is "admired by all who saw her" (v. 15). She easily wins the king's favor, and receives both a crown and a banquet. Overt and covert allusions to

Vashti abound as Esther accepts what her predecessor refused and becomes the next trophy wife.

Mordecai's good fortune seems to be as great as Esther's charm. Being in the right place at the right time, he discovers a plot against the king and intervenes to save his life. Though he had cautioned Esther not to reveal her nationality, he now conveys a warning to the king through Esther, risking the disclosure of their kinship.

What more compliant and loyal subjects could a king hope for than these two counterparts, Esther in the bedchamber and Mordecai at the gate? What commentary do their actions begin to suggest concerning Vashti, and what commentary does her action suggest concerning these two nearly assimilated Jews?

Key Terms

Eunuch: A castrated man placed in charge of a harem or employed as a chamberlain in a palace.

Almost parenthetically, and yet twice, we are told that Mordecai directs Esther to hide her ancestry. It is worthwhile to ponder the significance of this note of foreboding. Esther's story was written long before Roman and Christian anti-Semitism took root. The Persian empire was filled with small ethnic groups, each with its own language and customs. There was no known reason Jews would be particularly vulnerable. As the story progresses, the narrator

> "It is one thing to live a life that is faithful to God when one is surrounded by a culture that supports such efforts. It is quite another to remain faithful in a cultural context that is not similarly committed and that, in fact, may be openly hostile to the life of faith."
> Bechtel, *Esther*, 10.

will display a strong self-consciousness about Jewishness. But what exactly being Jewish entails in a book with no mention of either the Jewish God or Jewish customs is difficult to pinpoint.

A Fly in the Royal Ointment: Esther 3:1–6

After Esther is given Vashti's crown and Mordecai's lifesaving deed is recorded in the king's annals, we might reasonably expect that the two of them would be set up for life. In fact, chapter 3 begins promisingly: "After these things King Ahasuerus promoted . . ." But a sudden shift occurs: Someone else, another foreigner, is promoted. No reason is given for this, nor for the ego-enhancing vocational perk that accompanies it. But why should a king who has already demonstrated his capriciousness be obliged to justify the favors he grants? We are reminded, with Mordecai and Esther, that no degree of concern for the welfare and pleasure of an impulsive king can guarantee appropriate rewards—or even, we discover as the chapter unfolds, protection from death.

At this point, as the last major characters appear on stage, it is important to note how we come to know them. Their personalities are not directly described. We form our impressions not by imbibing the narrator's judgments but by "seeing" the characters' actions and "hearing" their words. That is to say, we get to know biblical characters in very much the same way that we get to know people in real life. By leaving judgment up to us, the narrator shows trust in our discernment and invites us to participate in the making of the story. As a result, even characters that are sparsely drawn spring to life like the characters in James Thurber's minimalist line drawings.

Ahasuerus was introduced in terms of his colossal glory, his infinite excess, his mercurial temper, and his confident reliance on subordinates to tell him what to do. Mordecai and Esther have so far not emerged clearly, and this may be exactly the effect they wish to evoke: Like other associates of the king, they seem more bent on pleasing the king than on attracting attention.

Haman's position is somewhere in between. Whereas Ahasuerus's glory flows from his position as king of the known universe, Haman's glory is a derivative stream, from his job as the king's lackey-in-chief. Still, his prestige is both considerable and hollow: By command of the king, all other servants must literally bow down before Haman. That is, if they want to keep their jobs, they must display deep respect for him, genuine or not.

Here is the moment at which Mordecai begins to stand out as an interesting protagonist. For unexplained reasons, Mordecai refuses to bow. As Bechtel points out, his refusal is not likely religious in nature, since even the most devout Israelites paid such homage to humans. Though ancestral "bad blood" between the two of them may lie somewhere near the root of this standoff, or perhaps resentment at being passed over for promotion, Mordecai is as silent about his reasons for not bowing to Haman as Vashti was for not appearing at the king's party. And just as Vashti's refusal resulted in rage, deliberation, and an edict against all the women in the land, Mordecai's refusal results in rage, deliberation, and an edict against all the Jews of the land.

Mordecai's slight doesn't bother Haman until it is pointed out by others. When it is, he becomes furious enough to destroy not just the one man who embarrasses him but all who fit his "racial profile."

Such overreaction is hardly new in Esther. The narrator's deadpan telling brings us face to face not just with folly but with its inherent violence. Esther may be a funny story, but it is also deeply horrifying.

A Word in the Royal Ear: Esther 3:7–15

As Bechtel notes, Haman casts lots not to determine the propitious day to make his request but the day to carry it out. He assumes that any day is a good day to ask the king to destroy his subjects. It turns out that he is right. Haman approaches the king with carefully crafted rhetoric, constructed of truths, half-truths, and downright lies. Certainly the Jews are scattered around the empire, but he makes it sound like a conspiracy. Certainly each group's norms and rules are different from those of all other groups, but Haman makes it sound as if all the other various peoples in the vast empire of Persia follow one set of rules and all the Jews follow another. One Jew, Mordecai, failed to keep one law, the law to bow down to Haman—hardly a mass movement. In saying, "It is not appropriate for the king to tolerate them," he transforms his own complaint about Mordecai into the king's problem with all the Jewish people, though he never informs the king that it is either Mordecai or the Jews that he is talking about.

> The casting of lots was a common method for determining the divine will in ancient Israel and in New Testament times. Yet no detailed description of the actual procedures involved or of the precise instruments used is offered in the Bible. Various notable events recorded in the Bible were determined by the casting of lots: Saul's selection as king (1 Sam. 10:16–26), the apportionment of conquered lands (Num. 26:55), and the division of Jesus' possessions by the soldiers who crucified him (Matt. 27:35).
>
> From Paul J. Achtemeier, ed., *HarperCollins Bible Dictionary*, rev. ed. (New York: HarperCollins, 1996), 624–25.

Perhaps fearing that rhetoric alone will not be convincing enough, he appeals to the king's greed, while insulting his honor, by offering a colossal bribe. In this gesture, Haman reveals himself as not only unimaginably wealthy but willing to spend enormous amounts of money to settle a very minor score. An Oskar Schindler in reverse, he throws away a personal fortune not to save the Jews but to destroy them.

How does the king respond? An extremely serious charge has been brought before him against an unidentified group, and a violent measure has been recommended that could throw his empire into civil war. The one advising him to do this has just revealed what a deep personal investment he has in seeing this group destroyed. Another leader might have assembled a fact-finding committee to investigate the charges, asked which group of people Haman wished to destroy and what laws they had broken, or at least had Haman arrested for attempted bribery.

However, in chapters 1 and 2 we already saw a repeated pattern of royal behavior: The king listens to advisors and agrees to what they say, rather quickly making large and not necessarily judicious policy decisions. Further, he takes a hands-off approach, allowing others to write the laws and carry them out. True to form, Ahasuerus once again accedes to the counsel of his advisor but declines to take an active part. He gives Haman his signet ring to write any edict he'd like, he gives him back the money, apparently to bankroll the operation, and he gives him the Jews, to do with whatever he wants. Searching hard for a positive spin, we might say this king does not micromanage his kingdom or his advisors, and he keeps his administrative meetings short and to the point.

> "The book of Esther is many things. . . . It is a tale of intrigue at court, a story of lethal danger to the Jews narrowly averted by heroic rescue. It is also a tale of the ascent of an orphan in exile to the rank of the most powerful woman—and perhaps even the most powerful person—in the empire and, arguably, the world. [It] is the story of how a humiliated and endangered minority . . . came to be respected and feared by the Gentile majority and to see one of their own honored by appointment to the second highest post in the empire. It is the comical story of a pompous fool who does himself in and the chilling tale of the narrow escape from death of a despised and ever-vulnerable minority. It is all these things and more, and readers who are satisfied that they know what Esther means would be well advised to examine it again in search of other dimensions." Levenson, *Esther*, 1.

Given all the power one man can imagine, Haman summons the king's secretaries, writes a decree in the name of the king, and sends it out. Notice of the decree, with its systematic listing of categories, its official language hardly disguising the horror, is at the same time farcical and horrific: "orders to destroy, to kill, and to annihilate all Jews, young and old, women and children, in one day, the thirteenth day of the twelfth month, which is the month of Adar, and to plunder their goods" (3:13).

As chilling as this episode is, there is still a strong element of the surreal to it. Haman has chosen a day eleven months in the future, a single day, to eradicate a people whose history is rooted in the origins of the world itself. He displays an ultimate confidence both in the effectiveness of royal decrees and in the law-abiding nature of Persians and Jews. He doesn't seem to expect the Jews to try to protect themselves. And he expects their non-Jewish neighbors to live peaceably side by side with them for eleven months, and then on the appointed day, to up and kill them. But the reactions in the empire are anything but orderly: "The king and Haman sat down to drink; but the city of Susa was thrown into confusion" (3:15). Things will not go as Haman plans.

Now we may begin to see how Vashti's cameo nonappearance functions in the story of Esther. In a rather gentler way, the narrator has used her to draw parallels. Though her noncompliance contrasts with Esther's pliability, it also foreshadows Mordecai's actions, suggesting that like Mordecai she did not need to be a habitual offender to fall out of favor with the king. Though Vashti could have been, like Mordecai, the king's most loyal ally, her safety rested not on her record but on the king's unpredictable temper. Both Vashti and Mordecai enrage someone who is politically powerful but personally insecure. They both do so by violating an outlandish royal command. The resulting punishment is inflicted not on them alone but on the entire group they are perceived as representing, in Vashti's case the women and in Mordecai's case the Jews. What happens to Vashti and Mordecai, and to those they are viewed as representing, establishes a firm parallel in the book between thoughtless contempt for women and thoughtless contempt for ethnic minorities.

 Want to Know More?

About the connections between Haman and Mordecai's ancestry? See Bechtel, *Esther*, 30.

About the casting of lots? See Paul J. Achtemeier, ed., *HarperCollins Bible Dictionary*, rev. ed. (New York: HarperCollins, 1996), 624–25.

Such parallels between racism and sexism are well known in our contemporary world. It is striking that such parallel sins should be so boldly described in an ancient narrative, written in a world not primarily known for its attention to such issues. This serves as a reminder not to assume that biblical views of gender and race are either predictable or objectionable.

The main characters have now been introduced and the plot set in motion. Both Ahasuerus and Haman have appeared in settings that emphasize their power and pomp. Yet each behaves in ways that prompt readers at the very least to question their fitness for the honors and responsibilities they have somehow amassed. At most, watching them sit down to a drinking bout together in the midst of the havoc they have created, we might ask with Jeremiah, "Why does the way of the guilty prosper? Why do all who are treacherous thrive?" (Jer. 12:1).

Mordecai and Esther remain indistinct for now. Their reward for saving the king's life has become a death sentence. But soon both of them will emerge from Susa's turmoil to take action.

? Questions for Reflection

1. Does it bother you that Esther seemed to be trying to gain the king's favor, even during this forced conscription of young women by the king? Why or why not?
2. Mordecai refused to bow down to Haman, and faced the consequences. Name some other people in history who refused to bow down to another and paid a price. How were their circumstances similar to or different from Mordecai's?
3. The author writes that the book of Esther "serves as a reminder not to assume that biblical views or gender and race are either predictable or objectionable." What do you think she means by this?
4. Throughout history there is a long record of persecution of the Jewish people, from ancient times to the Holocaust of the 1940s. Do you still believe anti-Semitism is widely practiced today? Have you seen it in your community? In your church?

Such a Time as This

The News Spreads: Esther 4:1–5

In this suspenseful segment of Esther, we learn how Mordecai and Esther respond to Haman's murderous decree. As chapter 3 ends and chapter 4 begins, several snapshots occur in quick succession. First, we see Haman and the king within the palace walls, privately celebrating their murder pact (3:15). Theirs is the book's fifth banquet; the next two, very different in character, will follow soon. Next we see three "outside" snapshots. The first is a panorama of the population of Susa, where pandemonium reigns (3:15). The second is a close-up of Mordecai, who adds his own voice to the general outcry (4:1–2). The third broadens to a sweeping gaze at the Jews throughout the empire, who are fasting, lamenting, and lying in sackcloth and ashes (4:3).

Our gaze returns finally to the palace, where we discover that the decree announced in the far corners of the land has not reached the queen's own quarters (4:4). She knows neither what is happening to her people, nor what her own husband has done.

What exactly Esther's maids and eunuchs tell her is not spelled out. Though at first it sounds as if they have told her everything, her response indicates she may only know the most superficial element of the story: Mordecai is at the gate "woefully out of compliance with the palace dress code" (Bechtel, 44). The motif of Mordecai's clothing that begins here will prove to be an important one as time goes on.

Esther sends her cousin clothing. What exactly this delightfully ambiguous gesture is meant to communicate goes unstated. Is Esther trying to fix Mordecai's sorrow by fixing his attire? Is she summoning him inside the gate with proper dress so they can confer? Exhorting him to show proper respect for the palace? Expressing the teenage cliche, "You are embarrassing me!"? Hoping to cover up his Jewish identity? Or is this just a gesture of panic, a denial of realities too frightening to allow?

Evidently judging her response inadequate, Mordecai refuses the garments without comment. Esther becomes the story's third person to receive a refusal conveyed by messengers. But unlike King Ahasuerus with Vashti, and Haman with Mordecai, who both reacted without inquiring, Esther wants to know, to translate the Hebrew literally, "what is this and what is it about."

"While Mordecai's grief is the focus of these two verses, the description is not so detailed as to probe into the specific reasons for his grief. While the main one is obvious—namely, the impending destruction of his people—we are left to wonder whether he feels any personal responsibility for their peril. . . . The text is resolutely silent about such ruminations, so interpreters must be content to leave such questions unanswered. (Part of the artistry of this book, however, is its knack for making us ask them!)" Bechtel, *Esther*, 45.

The Crucial Interchange: Esther 4:6–14

Esther sends one of the eunuchs, Hathach, to find out. Through his shuttling back and forth between her quarters and the outside world, Esther and Mordecai carry on an urgent and passionate conversation. Emphasis on the mediated nature of this conversation underscores the delicacy of her situation. All hope dangles from a tenuous thread. What if Hathach garbles the message? What if he is stopped? What if he betrays them?

This central conversation between Esther and her cousin Mordecai marks a turning point in their relationship. Until now, Mordecai has been Esther's protector. Everything he has told her to do has been for her protection. And Esther has indeed needed such protection. King Ahasuerus has not so far been merciful to either women or Jews, and Esther is both of these. But now Mordecai will reverse his protective role, and Esther is forced to grow up from childhood to adulthood.

Hathach finds Mordecai in the open square of the city. With relentless specificity, Mordecai conveys to Esther the exact sum of money Haman offered the king, demonstrating again his talent for uncovering the damning secrets of others. He gives Hathach a copy of the decree to show her, and unambiguous instructions to plead for "her people" before the king.

Esther seems poised to refuse. "All the king's servants and the people of the king's provinces know," she begins (4:11). Everyone knows, and he should too, the danger of approaching the king unbidden. She adds something Mordecai probably does not know: She hasn't been summoned by the king in a month, so odds are slim that she can wait for an invitation. As Bechtel points out (47), commentators have construed Esther's hesitation as cowardice or selfishness. Even Mordecai seems to construe it thus. But Esther has not refused yet. She has only clarified the probable consequences. Neither Vashti nor Mordecai should be blamed for occasioning harsh decrees by intemperate leaders. Still, after these results, Esther's pause to think before acting is worth noting.

Her words reveal yet another of the many arbitrary regulations in Esther's Persia. We have already seen several strange laws: laws of unrestrained drinking (1:8), queenly banishment and wifely obedience (1:22), virgin conscription and beautification (2:2–4, 12), subservient obeisance (3:2), legalized genocide (3:9–10), and palace dress codes (4:2). Now no one can come to the king unbidden. The plot will turn on more odd laws before it all ends.

Mordecai answers with his only direct speech of the whole book. He musters several arguments at once. Rather than deferring to her protest, he says that if she does not go she will die. He intertwines this warning with a confident prediction of salvation even without her help: "For if you keep silence at such a time as this, relief and deliverance will rise for the Jews from another quarter, but you and your father's family will perish." Then, much more positively, he continues: "Who knows? Perhaps you have come to royal dignity for just such a time as this" (4:14).

The hedges in Mordecai's speech are as important as its assertions. As Michael Fox has said, "He raises the possibility that even before events began sliding toward disaster, some force was preparing the way for deliverance. . . . He is confident that the Jewish people will survive but uncertain about how this will come about" (245). His modesty on the subject of divine providence, along with his faith in the effectiveness of timely action, could be very instructive to any believer attempting to interpret the ways of God.

Getting Ready Again to Meet the King: Esther 4:16–17

Esther's answer displays both courage and leadership: "Go, gather all the Jews to be found in Susa, and hold a fast on my behalf, and neither eat nor drink for three days, night or day. I and my maids will also fast as you do. After that I will go to the king, though it is against the law; and if I perish, I perish" (4:16). For the first time, Esther does not receive an order from Mordecai, but instead gives him an order, which he obeys.

"If there was any question about her courage before, surely her terse 'if I perish, I perish' put such questions to rest." Bechtel, *Esther*, 50.

From this moment on, Esther's relationship to the world around her changes. Relinquishing the passivity of youth, she takes charge. This is not something we might have expected from her. So far in the story all she has done is to please other people. Vashti had told the king "no," but Esther has appeared quite reasonably hesitant to say anything at all to him. Vashti had been banished for failing to appear when the king called her; now Esther must appear before the king when he has not called her, and convince him to reverse the decree of his highest official.

"Verse 16 reads like a battle plan, and she is clearly the general. Indeed, Mordecai seems to recognize this role reversal first of all. Verse 17 attests to this with its laconic conclusion: 'Mordecai then went away and did everything as Esther had ordered him.'" Bechtel, *Esther*, 50.

This desperate situation calls for Esther to be "wise as a serpent and innocent as a dove" (Matt. 10:16). She takes three routes. First, she secures the support of the Jews in Susa, then she takes time to think it all through. Finally, she makes contrastive preparations: For three days she fasts, preparing her heart, but she dresses festively for her encore performance at "pleasing the king" in the only way this particular king seems to understand.

Other Tales

It was mentioned in chapter 1 that the book of Esther has survived in three closely related but distinct versions. These are: (1) the Hebrew version that became scripture for Jews and Protestants; (2) the Greek Septuagint version, which was scripture for the early church and continues, with adaptations, among Catholics today; and (3) the Alpha Text (or A-Text), which is found in a few ancient Greek manuscripts but not in any religious group's canon. Interesting distinctions among these versions appear throughout the book. Some of the most intriguing differences occur here.

As has already been observed, in the version of Esther shared by Jews and Protestants, God is never mentioned by either the narrator or the characters. Neither of the other versions shows such reticence with religious language, though they discuss God in different ways and at different times. In their conversation as Protestants know it, Mordecai and Esther refer to God only indirectly, if at all—Mordecai by citing "another quarter" from which deliverance might come and by suggesting that Esther's fortunes have a purpose (4:13–14); Esther by requesting a fast, an action normally accompanied by prayer (v. 16). But in the A-Text these speeches refer explicitly to God:

> Mordecai: "If you neglect to help your people, then *God will be their help and salvation,* but you and your father's house will perish."

> Esther: "Proclaim a *service of worship and pray earnestly to God*; and I and my handmaids will do likewise." (Clines, 227)

The Septuagint, unlike the A-Text, coincides with the Hebrew almost exactly in these two speeches. But immediately following this scene, the Septuagint adds two lengthy sections, known as "Addition C" and "Addition D." Readers who have an NRSV Bible with an Apocrypha will be able to find this "Greek Version of Esther" with its additions.

In Addition C, Mordecai and Esther each offer lengthy prayers for deliverance. Mordecai discloses religious motives for refusing to bow to Haman. Esther likewise protests her dislike for the king and palace life. In Addition D, after Esther finishes her prayers, an elaborate narration of the throne room scene commences. Whereas in the Hebrew version the king welcomes Esther immediately upon seeing her (5:2), the Septuagint lengthens the suspense to sixteen rather maudlin verses, in which she prays once again, takes two maids with her, sees the king looking majestic and terrifying, and faints. God intervenes, changing the king's spirit, and he springs from his throne to comfort her with soothing words. She flatters him and faints once again before the detour rejoins the more familiar narrative and the king offers to give her whatever she wants.

Readers respond differently to these additions. Some enjoy the extra details; others resist them, saying they leave too little to the imagination. The Greek additions are certainly born of a different kind of literary imagination than the Hebrew version. These differing styles give modern readers a window into scripture's complex history of development, and tease us with questions about Esther's origins.

Pleasing the King Once Again: Esther 5:1–8

In all three versions, Esther once again wins the king's favor. His response is the stuff of fairy tales: "What is your request? It shall be given you, even to the half of my kingdom" (5:3). Given that all the Jews in Persia are somewhat less than half the kingdom, it might at first glance appear as if Esther's problems are solved. But both we and Esther know the king's mercurial moods and capacity for changing his mind. We also know that Haman is the king's most influential and dangerous official, fully capable of thwarting her request and manipulating the king against her. So she first makes a request that is clearly safe: "If it pleases the king, let the king and Haman come today to a banquet that I have prepared for the king" (5:4). Of course, Esther always pleases the king, and the king never turns down a banquet, so naturally he agrees.

He calls for Haman, saying, "Bring Haman quickly, so that we may do as Esther desires" (5:5). Literally the Hebrew says, "so we may

Esther feasts with the King

do the word of Esther." This is a deliciously ironic twist on a king who only three chapters before was terrified that women might not do the word of their husbands. Vashti was banished for not coming when the king called, but now Esther has gotten away with coming when the king did not call. The king who worried about women obeying their husbands is now obeying his

wife, and ordering Haman to obey her as well. And to add irony to irony, Haman not only obeys a woman, but delights in being hosted by a Jew—a Jew passing as a Persian so splendidly that she puts the lie to all he said about her people's disruptiveness. This Jewish woman's invitation to two Gentile VIPs begins erasing the boundaries of who may eat and drink together in Esther's Persia. Power banquets will never be the same again.

Even the king realizes that Esther didn't risk her life just to invite the guys to lunch. So during the banquet, he asks her again what she really wants, reiterating twice as elaborately as before that he will give her half his kingdom. She replies, "This is my petition and request:

If I have won the king's favor, and if it pleases the king to grant my petition and fulfill my request, let the king and Haman come tomorrow to the banquet that I will prepare for them, and then I will do as the king has said" (5:7–8).

This speech warrants close examination. The king has reiterated his earlier promise, doubling everything he said before. On the surface, Esther appears to be repeating herself as well, issuing another invitation to another banquet. But when her speech is carefully examined, it becomes clear that she has actually thrown in something new. In essence she asks the king to sign a blank check: If you are indeed agreeing to grant my petition, come again tomorrow, when you will find out what you have agreed to. She even poses it as the favor she is doing for him.

Is all this necessary? The king has already stated twice, publicly, his intention to give Esther whatever she wants. Yet as fickle as the king's pleasure seems to be, an elaborate commitment, made in actions as well as words, is wise to secure, especially when the king learns that her request involves repudiating his highest official. Esther's caution is appropriate to the situation's gravity and the king's volatility.

Some modern people express discomfort with Esther's cleverness, accusing her of manipulation. It should be recalled, however, how Haman presented his case to the king: with lies, misstatements, and bribes. Esther uses none of these. Her banquet is no bribe, but a prelude to posing her request. And her goal is not death, but life. She marshals every resource possible, including good looks and savvy royal psychology, in the hopes of saving her people.

Want to Know More?

About the three versions of Esther? See Moore, *Esther,* lxi–lxiii. For a complete translation of the Alpha Text, see Clines, *Esther Scroll.*

About all six additions to Esther in the Greek Version? See Bechtel, *Esther,* 85–98.

Given the situation, Esther is certainly, as Mordecai points out, the right person in the right place at the right time. She has been called there by the king, but Mordecai hints that divine providence is the real impetus behind events. We can almost hear in his words the famous speech of Joseph, who rose to power in Egypt as a result of his brothers' treachery: "You meant evil against me; but God meant it for good, to bring it about that many people should be kept alive, as they are today" (Gen. 50:20 RSV).

Yet how much is Esther in control of her plans? Not knowing her thoughts, readers cannot discern whether she planned these three separate encounters from the start, whether she is awaiting the opportune moment, or whether she is simply showing hesitation. As it turns out, these delays allow time for other forces beyond Esther's control to play themselves out. A great deal is going to happen in the next twenty-four hours. Only in retrospect will it be clear how much providence has been at work.

? Questions for Reflection

1. What do you think Esther's reasons were for sending clothing to Mordecai? Why did he refuse it?
2. Though God is never mentioned in the book of Esther, 4:14 does carry an air of divine intervention. Do you think the writer intended this? Why or why not?
3. In this passage we see a sudden change in Esther's attitude to the world around her, as she prepares to go against the prevailing forces and norms. When in your life have you had to make such a sudden change? Why did you do it? What was the outcome?
4. Find a Bible with the Apocrypha and read the Greek additions to Esther. Do you prefer the story with them or without them? Why?

Plots, Parades, and Providence

Haman's Ups and Downs: Esther 5:9–16

A subtle but important feature of the narrative style in Esther is the selective access readers are given to the inner lives of Esther and her acquaintances. Even when the action shifts to the queen and she begins to execute her plans, not one glimpse is given into her emotions and thoughts. Rather, everything must be inferred from her actions. Haman's secret thoughts, on the other hand, are aired with some regularity, rendering him embarrassingly transparent.

After dining with the king and queen, Haman leaves Esther's banquet "happy and in good spirits" (5:9). His private audience with the royal couple has evidently left his hunger for prestige temporarily sated. But immediately he runs into Mordecai, who still neither rises nor trembles before him, and his emotions take a nosedive. Indeed, a major motif surrounding Haman, which will unfold especially in chapters 6 and 7, is the motif of high and low, up and down, both figuratively and literally.

Mordecai's simple act of ignoring Haman holds great power, dissolving his good mood. This brief encounter speaks worlds about what underlies Haman's violent intentions. His determination to destroy Mordecai's people arises from an ego so fragile it cannot survive any challenge, real or imagined. With cruel artistry the narrator follows the crushed Haman home and allows us to witness a conversation with his wife Zeresh and his friends. Horror and humor merge in this discussion, as the second most important personage in the known world reinflates his ego by rehearsing to his supporters, including his wife, "the splendor of his riches, the number of his sons,

29

all the promotions with which the king had honored him, and how he had advanced him above the officials and the ministers of the king" (5:11).

Haman is painfully unaware of his own diseased vision. Oblivious to Esther's plans for his defeat, Haman boasts that he alone was honored by an invitation to dine with the queen and the king. His offhand announcement, "Tomorrow also I am invited by her, together with the king," in which he makes himself the subject of Esther's honor and the king a parenthetical addendum, reverses the emphases in Esther's own invitation: "let the king come—and Haman—to a banquet which I have prepared for the king" (5:4, author's translation).

> "The real irony here is that Mordecai is already a condemned man. All Haman has to do is wait for the edict to take effect, and Mordecai (along with the rest of the Jews) will be out of his hair forever. But patience is not one of Haman's virtues (if indeed he has any). A year, evidently, is too long to wait when one's ego is being assailed. Only a special public humiliation on an accelerated schedule will do." Bechtel, *Esther*, 56.

Confirming the portrait furnished by the narrator earlier on the street, Haman goes on to complain to his supporters that "all this does me no good as long as I see the Jew Mordecai sitting at the king's gate" (5:13). Though he emphasizes "the Jew Mordecai," we know that the main point of contention is "the Jew Mordecai sitting." His wife and friends propose the obvious solution for someone who has nearly everything he wants: Rid Haman's world of this offender!

True to the excesses of the narrative in general, the mode of execution these alter egos of Haman's suggest represents, literally, overkill. Mordecai should be hung (or impaled, see Bechtel, 55), not just high enough to do the job but eight stories high, so that everyone in the city can see. Like the king in chapters 1 and 2, Haman appreciates and agrees to the advice of his support network. Since Mordecai will not rise *up* to bow *down*, and Mordecai's actions *lower* Haman's *high* spirits, Mordecai must be strung *up* fifty cubits high, and that will *raise* Haman's spirits.

> A cubit was the standard ancient Near Eastern linear measure. Theoretically it encompassed the distance from the elbow to the tip of the middle finger, about 17.5 to 20 inches.
>
> From Paul J. Achtemeier, ed., *HarperCollins Bible Dictionary*, rev. ed. (New York: HarperCollins, 1996), 213.

If Haman has his way, Esther's intervention the next day will come too late to save her own cousin. However, an important biblical theme, very much related to Haman's highs and lows, is the theme of reversal, of divine justice turning power upside down. This theme is so pervasive in the

Bible, and so commonplace in Christian discourse, that its radical implications can sometimes be forgotten.

Explicit reversals characterize many Proverbs, such as 16:18: "Pride goes before destruction, and a haughty spirit before a fall." Reversals also permeate narratives, such as the story of Joseph and his brothers (Gen. 37–50), the exodus of the Israelites from Egypt (Exod. 1–15), and the poem of Isaiah's suffering servant who will be exalted (Isa. 52:13–53:12). The narrative of reversal best known to Christians, of course, is the story of Jesus' death and resurrection.

Reversal will be pointed out explicitly toward the end of Esther, when the day that Haman's edict is to be executed is called "the very day when the enemies of the Jews hoped to gain power over them, but which had been changed to a day when the Jews would gain power over their foes" (9:1). That verse summarizes events that begin to take shape in chapter 6.

A Comedy of Mismatched Intentions: Esther 6:1–12

Haman's renewed indignation at Mordecai and his friends' rash suggestion to kill him are complications Esther could not have predicted, events threatening to undermine her patient cultivation of the king. But what happens next is something else Esther could not have predicted or planned. The highly surreal chapter 6 is heavy with coincidence. Reading the story in the biblical context, we might well claim not coincidence but providence: God's invisible hand seems to be at work behind the scenes.

The surreal series of providential coincidences runs as follows. It is the middle of the night and King Ahasuerus cannot sleep. So he does what many do for insomnia—he reads. Or rather, because he is king, he has servants read to him. Does he choose his own annals because they are his favorite story? Or his favorite sedative? What is read banishes sleep for the night, when he realizes he never rewarded the man who saved his life back in chapter 2. The king has a problem that must be solved.

Just then he hears something. We are told, a split second before the king finds out, that "Haman had just entered the outer court of the king's palace to speak to the king about having Mordecai hanged on the gallows that he had prepared for him" (6:4). This information establishes us as informed observers. In the scene that unfolds, neither the king nor Haman knows what the other is thinking. But we, having heard both Haman's conversation with his friends and the king's conversation with his servants, know far more than either of them does. We know they both have Mordecai on their minds. We know their intentions toward Mordecai are mutually contradictory. We know that neither of them is aware of the other's intention. We also know that, kings being kings, Haman is about to make a very unwelcome discovery.

"Of all the passages in the court record, the servant just happens to turn to the story of how Mordecai saved the king's life. It is there in all its glorious detail; even the names of the would be assassins are duly recorded. This is hardly the kind of bedtime reading that is likely to lull the king to sleep. Now wide awake he asks, 'What honor or distinction has been bestowed on Mordecai for this?' And the servants bluntly reply, 'Nothing has been done for him.'" Bechtel, *Esther*, 57.

The king speaks first. As usual, he seeks counsel: "'What shall be done for the man whom the king wishes to honor?'" (6:6). Haman, as usual, jumps to a conclusion, and the narrator, as usual, whispers to us Haman's private thoughts: "Haman said to himself, 'Whom would the king wish to honor more than me?'"

Haman's advice unfolds for readers on several levels. First, the sheer repetition of phrasing demands attention. "The man whom the king wishes to honor," said once by Ahasuerus, is repeated in Haman's speech three times in three verses (6:7–9), ending with the suggestion that it be repeated many more times in the street. Haman simply seems to love this phrase.

Second, we note the emptiness of the honor he proposes. What he suggests is nothing useful or practical—not a cash reward, not employment or security, certainly not a reversal of the edict of death that is Mordecai's actual most pressing need. Rather, Haman suggests the reward he himself would most enjoy: to parade the streets as king for a day.

Third, Haman's speech exposes yet again his increasingly rapacious ego. Tension mounts for readers, who know well that the "man whom the king wishes to honor" is not the one who is putting his foot further into his mouth with every phrase. How will he react when all is revealed?

We know what is coming next. Still, every extra word in the king's order, rubbing salt in Haman's wounded ego, adds to readerly delight: "*Quickly*, take the robes and the horse, *as you have said*, and do so to *the Jew* Mordecai *who sits at the king's gate. Leave out nothing that you have mentioned*" (6:10). The narrator relentlessly plunges ahead with repetitions, informing us in words echoing Haman's that Haman has done for Mordecai all these things he wanted for himself, and especially emphasizing the proclamation, "Thus shall it be done for the man whom the king wishes to honor" (6:11).

As Haman confirms his position as king's chief lackey by following the letter of his own advice to the king, his mood could not have been hospitable. In fact, the A-Text version describes Mordecai's terror when Haman approaches him at the city gate with the command, "Take off the sackcloth" (see Clines, 237).

Mordecai and Haman

This is the second time clothing has been brought out to Mordecai from the palace. Though it is the king's royal robe, a garment coveted by Haman, its sudden and temporary appearance as the costume commanded for a condemned man must have seemed ironic at best, mocking at worst. We are not told what Mordecai thinks of being made to participate in this spectacle. He submits himself to the event and then returns to the gate. But Haman's feelings are clear for everyone on the streets to see, as he hurries to his house, mourning and with his head covered.

Collapse of the Support Network: Esther 6:13–14

As soon as Haman goes home he does exactly what he did the last time his ego bruised itself against Mordecai. He summons his wife and his supporters once again. This time the narrator doesn't enumerate his boasts but rushes through his complaint: Haman tells "everything that had happened to him" (6:13)—as if he had been an innocent bystander minding his own business, suddenly victimized by the king's disgraceful treatment.

Haman's wife and friends (now called *chachamav*, "his wise men"), mirroring his despondency, reverse their earlier position. They note that Haman has begun to fall before Mordecai, and predict that his final downfall is inevitable. Interestingly, they seem to base this prediction not on anything in Haman or his behavior, nor on the king's reaction, but on Mordecai's Jewishness, a factor they knew but did not acknowledge the previous day. Some kind of numinous power seems to be imputed to Jews by Haman's friends. Once again the theme of high and low is evident: Since Haman could not string Mordecai *up*, Haman has begun his *downfall*, and will surely *fall* before Mordecai.

> "Circumstances seem to have conspired against Haman, and for once, we get the impression he is completely unprepared. Esther, however, is not. The chapter closes with a reference to the banquet that she has prepared. We can be sure that her preparations involve far more than food." Bechtel, *Esther*, 61.

On this final point they are ironically mistaken. Before they finish speaking, the king's officials arrive and hurry Haman off to Esther, before whom his most literal downfall will soon take place.

Coincidence or Providence?

We must pause at the doorway of Esther's quarters to consider cause and effect. In speaking to the king the previous day, Esther set a chain of events into motion. Though she acted with courage, shrewdness, and self-restraint, several events have happened to further her plan, events she had no role in orchestrating. She did not cause Haman to swell with pride because he dined with the queen, nor did she engineer the encounter with Mordecai that ruined his good mood. She did not cause Haman's wife and friends to suggest killing Mordecai, and she did not initiate Haman's trip to the palace to demand an execution. Nor did she plan the king's insomnia, his reading of the episode concerning Mordecai, or his desire to repay him. And she certainly had no responsibility for the deft way in which Haman arranged a parade to honor himself, only to be forced to honor Mordecai instead.

Want to Know More?

About whether a noose or stake was the instrument of execution? See Bechtel, *Esther*, 55.

Esther's seemingly impossible task has been rendered easier and easier by all these events. Haman has been deeply insulted and frightened, the king has been reminded of his debt to Mordecai, and evidence of Haman's hatred stands several stories high in his backyard. It seems Esther has had some help. But what sort of help was it? We might ask of Haman's downfall, paraphrasing the words of Jesus, "Did it come from heaven, or was it of human origin?" (see Matt. 21:25). Haman's own indomitable presumptuousness has certainly come to Esther's assistance, aided by the king's habit of seeking advice and the fickleness of Haman's friends. But all of these together still cannot account for everything that happened, particularly the fortuitous timing of the king's insomnia, the selection of bedtime stories, and his sudden awareness of the unpaid debt to Mordecai. In a much magnified and telescoped way, things just worked themselves out. The planets lined up just right. Or God was at work behind the scenes.

Haman's edict still stands. Haman still holds office as "one of the king's most noble officials" (6:9), as affirmed by the king's selecting him to honor Mordecai. The Jews are still condemned. The king has not heard Esther's petition. Yet even before Haman's friends finish warning him, the plot rushes Haman to the next scene, Esther's second banquet, where Haman's goose will be cooked.

 ## Questions for Reflection

1. Have you ever had to deal with someone like Haman, with "an ego so fragile it cannot survive any challenge, real or imagined?" What strategies do you have for interactions with people like this?
2. Esther had to show much courage in her dealings with Haman. Has there been a time in your life when you've felt like Esther must have felt? Have you ever felt like Haman?
3. There is much coincidence and/or divine intervention in the story of Esther, Mordecai, Haman, and King Ahasuerus. Can you think of a time in your life when coincidence felt like divine intervention?
4. Haman and Mordecai were clearly rivals, though exactly why isn't ever fully explained. Do you have a rival in your life? How do you treat each other? Do you know why you became rivals?

5 Esther 7:1–8:17

Counterplots and Counter-edicts

Feasting Once Again: Esther 7:1–4

Chapter 7 of Esther begins right where the previous chapter ended. The king's eunuchs had gathered Haman to Esther's feast—an ominous note, as Bechtel points out, given what happened to Vashti, the last person summoned through the eunuchs to a feast. The first verse says literally, "And the king came, and Haman, to drink with Esther the queen." This is Esther's second banquet, the book's seventh, and they get right down to the drinking. Perhaps the rattled Haman, fresh from his humiliating parade with Mordecai and dressing down at home, finds a drink from the queen's hands most welcome.

Esther, Haman, and the King

Repeating his previous speech nearly verbatim, the king asks once again what Esther wants. What he may lack in imagination, he more than makes up for in persistence. This is an important repetition, however, because a whole day has passed since he asked before. He has had a chance to sleep on his extravagant offer (or, as the case may be, *not* to sleep on it), and he is still repeating it.

Esther is ready for him. If Haman's movements can be described as sharp ups and downs, Esther's resemble a gentle spiral. In repeated conversations, she circles round and round the king's repeated promise, and with each turn her prospects rise. The king remains stationary, repeating himself over and over, each time more formally and elaborately. But she has done something different with every response. First, she extended hospitality. Then she promised to tell him what she wanted if he would commit himself by coming to her second party. Now, fully positioned for a favorable hearing, she unveils her shocking request.

She mirrors the king very directly, using his vocabulary of petition and request: "If I have won your favor, O king, and if it pleases the king, let my life be given me—that is my petition—and the lives of my people—that is my request" (v. 3). Then she breaks with his words completely and begins instead to repeat the language of Haman's edict: "For we have been sold, I and my people, to be destroyed, to be killed, and to be annihilated" (v. 4). Here the modern translations, while presenting her speech in grammatical English, cannot quite capture the Hebrew, which precisely repeats the edict. According to Esther 3:13, the edict was sent "giving orders to destroy, to kill, and to annihilate all Jews. . . ." Esther repeats, "For we have been sold, I and my people, to destroy and to kill and to annihilate."

Esther's sentence at the end of verse 4 is masterfully ambiguous—so ambiguous, in fact, that nearly every modern translation renders it differently. She claims that if there had been a lesser evil, if enslavement rather than murder had been the danger, she would not have spoken up. In the rest of the verse, confusion reigns. The subject is either "the enemy" or "the affliction"; the predicate is either "will not compensate for," "is not worthy of," "cannot be compared with," or "cannot justify"; and the object of the sentence is either "the king's trouble," "annoyance to the king," or "damage to the king." Any combination of these variables is possible, and the range of acceptable translations is well exemplified by the following:

> "[Esther] is patient in implementing her plan of attack. She is brilliant in her analysis of her enemy's methods. And finally, she is every bit his equal in her power to persuade. Esther's character is so strong by the end of this chapter that we almost begin to feel sorry for Haman. But not quite. In the words of Jane Austen—another author famous for her strong female characters—Haman has 'delighted us long enough' (*Pride and Prejudice*, ch. 18). We are glad to see him go." Bechtel, *Esther*, 67.

NRSV: "but no enemy can compensate for this damage to the king"
NIV: "because no such distress would justify disturbing the king"
TANAKH: "for the adversary is not worthy of the king's trouble"

While it is possible that an originally clear intent has somehow been muddied by accidental ambiguity, it is also possible that this final flourish of diplomatic obscurity was fully intended. The original audience, hearing the story in Hebrew, would not have had to choose among the interpretive options but would have enjoyed hearing the full range in a single deliciously indistinct phrase.

Falling Once Again: Esther 7:5–10

Ahasuerus, who had no idea of either his wife's lineage or her endangerment, is not at all prepared for her speech. His question fairly sputters with surprised indignation: "Who is he, and where is he, who has presumed to do this?" (7:5). He is the only person who does not know the answer. The audience anticipates it; surely a stupefied Haman dreads it. "A foe and enemy, this wicked Haman," Esther states (7:6). She has successfully positioned the king with herself and over against her enemy. Haman realizes this too, and he is terrified for his life.

The enraged king storms from the room. For a moment it is not clear what this means. Is he angry at the queen for her accusation? Is he furious with the stunningly revealed intentions of his official? Is he trying to calm down, seek advice, or avoid a decision between his two closest subjects? As Adele Berlin points out, from a literary perspective, he must leave the room to set the stage for what happens next (69).

Now it is Haman's turn to plead for his life. Ironically, he chooses to plead not with his friend the king but with the woman he has so recklessly endangered, the one for whose cousin a fifty-cubit scaffolding stands waiting outside. Again Haman's theme song can be heard: He *stands up* to approach the queen in order, we are told, to plead for his life, and her husband returns just in time to watch him *fall down* on her couch. Esther, wisely, says nothing at all.

"Will he even assault the queen in my presence, in my own house?" exclaims King Ahasuerus (7:8). Is his misapprehension deliberate or accidental? We cannot tell. If it is accidental, the king's own self-absorption comes to the fore (my queen, my house, my presence), obscuring his judgment. If it is deliberate, it is certainly convenient. He can now justify punishing Haman for treason—not the treason of murdering the king's subjects (an act for which the king himself shares culpability) but the treason of usurping the king's bed, a believable accusation against a man who has managed to receive the king's signet ring and has angled to wear the king's clothes and ride the king's horse. In the end, the man who attempted to kill a people for a crime they did not commit will himself die for a crime he did not commit. Haman's lust was for power, not pleasure, but that is probably not the story his poor wife will hear.

Harbona, one of the ubiquitous eunuchs sent out to fetch Vashti in the opening chapter, knows something the king in his palace apparently does not. Before Ahasuerus even has the chance to seek advice, Harbona directs his attention to the damning evidence towering above the city: "Look, the very gallows that Haman has prepared for Mordecai, whose word saved the king, stands at Haman's house, fifty cubits high" (7:9). This time the king catches the drift before the suggestion is spelled out. "Hang him on that," he says, and that is that. As Bechtel says, adapting the words of Jane Austen, "Haman has 'delighted us long enough.' We are glad to see him go" (67).

Pleading Once Again: Esther 8:1–17

The action in chapter 7 moves so precipitously, and Haman falls so decisively, that the audience may be tempted, along with the king, to consider the danger past and the remainder a mere sorting out of rewards, as the music swells and the credits roll up the screen. Esther is quickly given the domicile of the man who had tried to destroy and despoil the Jews. Mordecai takes his rightful place in the court as the king's in-law. One transaction leads to another in quick succession. Haman's property passes from the king to the queen to her cousin. The king passes to Mordecai, like a hot potato, the powerful signet ring he has just taken from Haman's hand, the ring that had been used literally to seal the fate of the Jews but that had served instead to seal the fate of its user. Negative parallels between Haman and Mordecai, sharpened in chapter 6 when Mordecai received the reward intended for Haman, and in chapter 7 when Haman received the sentence

> "There is a kind of 'all's well that ends well' feeling at the end of verse 2. Perhaps Ahasuerus thinks he has done enough for one day, or indeed, has done all that needs to be done. Esther has Haman's house, after all, and Mordecai has the king's own signet ring. What more could they want?" Bechtel, *Esther*, 69.

intended for Mordecai, are reinforced as Mordecai finally inherits the job he arguably deserved back in chapter 2.

The one thing the king seems to forget is the one thing that matters: He has not granted the petition Esther so carefully crafted, the one he had promised three times. Mordecai and Esther are being heaped with rewards, but their lives are still in danger. When in verse 3 Esther begins to plead once again with the king, we are not told whether she is speaking up immediately or after some time. What does become obvious is that she no longer must comport herself with reserve. Her dramatic performance startles us into recognizing that relationships around the king have shifted decisively. Neither fasting nor dressing nor hesitating, she falls at his feet to plead before he can even react. When he repeats the earlier gesture with the scepter, we are quickly reminded of the contrasts between Esther's terror before and her confidence now. She stands and, after four deferential introductions, gets to her point: Please revoke the edict of death. Correctly presuming her own safety, she bases her argument this time not on the king's advantage or pleasure but on her own distress. For once, the king hears an argument founded not on his own gain but on the good of his subjects.

He begins by rehearsing what he has already done, and at first it is not clear where his speech will go. He replies to Esther and to Mordecai, "'I have given Esther the house of Haman, and they have hanged him on the gallows, because he plotted to lay hands on the Jews'" (8:7). The next sentence could be, "How can you ask for more?" Or, it could be, "Why doubt that I would grant you this as well?" Instead, his response is astounding feeble, especially for someone who has just exercised the power to transfer both personal and professional property in enormous proportions from one subject to another: "You may write as you please with regard to the Jews, in the name of the king, and seal it with the king's ring; for an edict written in the name of the king and sealed with the king's ring cannot be revoked" (8:8).

As Bechtel says, "Now we are truly incredulous about how free Ahasuerus has been with his signet ring" (71), a ring so powerful that not even the emperor of the known world can undo what it has done. We may ask, "Who

> "More striking even than Ahasuerus's lack of imagination is his lack of power. One cannot help but compare the "Mighty Man" of the book's introduction with the weak and ineffectual monarch pictured here. . . . One thing, at least, is clear. Esther and Mordecai cannot rely on Ahasuerus for much help. The words of a dead traitor have proven more powerful than the commands of a living king. Their only option seems to be to fight fire with fire—edict with edict." Bechtel, *Esther*, 72.

enacted such a silly law, and who will enforce it?" But neither the king nor his two subjects question the terrible law's wisdom or finality.

Instead, Mordecai gets to work. As a plot device, the irrevocable edict makes room for a parallel counter-edict. Simple revocation would have been preferred, and would certainly have been less confusing and bloody. But like the good fairies in *Sleeping Beauty* when faced with the irrevocable curse, Mordecai fashions wording that will do the job. In language clearly reminiscent of, and yet more specific than, larger than, and delivered on horses faster than Haman's edict, the Jews are allowed to nullify the edict of death by defending themselves.

An ambiguity appears in the terms of Mordecai's edict, an ambiguity reflected in the Hebrew as well as in some, but not all, English translations. Permission is given for the Jews "to destroy, to kill, and to annihilate any armed force of any people or province that might attack them, *with their children and women,* and to plunder their goods" (8:11). It is not clear whose children and women are referred to. Is it the families of the attackers, who are being declared fair game? Or is it the families of those attacked, since Haman's edict had ordered the destruction of "all Jews, young and old, women and children"? The two possibilities read very differently. There is no indication in the ensuing narrative that anyone but the attackers are killed. Still, the ambiguity reminds us of the horror Haman intended, which could have been returned. Permission is also given to take their enemies' plunder, but it will be stated three times in the narrative that follows (9:10, 15, 16) that the Jews declined to take the plunder, a move demonstrating their aim as self-defense, not greed.

In the final three verses of chapter 8, a direct reversal of the events following Haman's decree occurs. The final sentence of chapter 3 had read, "The king and Haman sat down to drink; but the city of Susa was thrown into confusion" (3:15). Here, however, rather than sitting down to drink with the king in isolation, Mordecai leaves the king to emerge from the palace to the street, where the city of Susa rings not with distress but with joy. He wears royal robes of blue and white,

> "Modern Christians may read this 'good news' with mixed emotions. We neither can nor should forget Jesus' words about turning the other cheek and loving our enemies. Yet we must also try to read this story on its own terms even as we read it within its broader canonical context. Crucial to the latter is the recognition that violence was not Esther and Mordecai's first choice. . . . Believers in every age must make such choices." Bechtel, *Esther,* 76.

with a great golden crown and a mantle of fine linen. He has come a long way from the sackcloth of chapter 3 and the temporary king costume of chapter 6—he has royalty of his own now.

This eighth festival, rising up from below, along with the two more that will quickly follow in chapter 9, stands in stark contrast to the three feasts with which the story began. It celebrates good fortunes rather than the king's fortune. In fact, rather than drawing artificial dividing lines between men and women, nobles and commoners, this celebration invites all who will enter into its spirit. According to the last line of the chapter, many Gentiles that day decide it is high time to join the Jews.

The story could end here with hardly any damage to its substance. In fact, some scholars suggest that the story originally did end here, with one edict nullified by the other. What follows in the final two chapters ensues many months later. It both explains the festival of Purim and, for many, raises questions about how such a fanciful story, with horror and humor so delicately balanced against each other, should end.

 Questions for Reflection

1. The author writes that the obscure nature of Esther's words in 7:4 is "masterfully ambiguous" and may have been intended. What might have been some of the reasons for this deliberate ambiguity?

2. Some would say that what happened to Haman was poetic justice. Do you think poetic justice ever happens in the real world, or just in the movies and fairy tales? Discuss some specific instances.

3. Esther had to throw herself on the king's mercy to show him the seriousness of the situation. Have you ever had to throw yourself on someone's mercy in order to open their eyes to a situation of injustice?

4. The author writes that "the story could end here [8:17] with hardly any damage to its substance." Do you agree, or is there more that needs to be said?

Dueling Decrees and Purim Parties

By the beginning of chapter 9, the roles of all around Ahasuerus have been reversed. Esther has moved from Vashti's place as trophy wife to a position of authority and respect. Rather than hosting an adjunct banquet of palace women, she has caused celebration of women and men, young and old, throughout the known world. The king's arrogant advisor Haman has been cast down, and the Jew Mordecai at the city gate has been exalted. The ending in chapters 9–10, relating events several months later when the two conflicting edicts come into effect, brings to thorough completion all that has been set into motion. Once again there is a day of reversals: "the very day when the enemies of the Jews hoped to gain power over them, but which had been changed to a day when the Jews would gain power over their foes" (9:1).

The conclusion of Esther causes many people uneasiness. Its style and vision are so different from the rest of the book that many scholars think it may have been added by someone other than the author of the previous chapters. The earlier chapters' keen sense of justice and aesthetics are not so distinct in the book's conclusion. Yet theological gold can be mined from the very fact of its complexity.

Three Endings

Chapter 9 concerns two general subjects: the fighting between the Jews and their enemies in the month of Adar, and the institution of Purim to commemorate the Jews' rest from conflict. Chapter

> "Esther is true to real life as it is lived messily with loose ends and threads coming undone." Van Wijk-Bos, *Ruth and Esther*, 116.

10 concludes with further information on the reign of King Ahasuerus and his new right-hand man Mordecai.

Chapter 9 is filled with inconsistencies and redundancies. At points it reads as if several endings had been tacked together by an uncertain editor. The plot of the story is recapitulated in verses 24–25 with facts differing just enough to be disconcerting. Commenting on Esther's "ragged ending," Johanna W. H. van Wijk-Bos notes that life itself rarely has tidy endings: "Esther is true to real life as it is lived messily with loose ends and threads coming undone" (116).

This ending is made even more interesting by the history of Esther's transmission. As we have explored in earlier chapters, three different versions of Esther have been passed down in history side by side. The differences among these versions is nowhere more striking than in Esther's ending.

In the version found in Jewish and Protestant Bibles, the thirteenth day of the twelfth month finally arrives and, as Mordecai's decree had authorized, the Jews gather and defend themselves. Five hundred enemies die in Susa, as well as Haman's ten sons. King Ahasuerus reports to Esther concerning the battles and asks her what she wants now. Without preliminaries, she requests an extra day of battle in Susa and asks that Haman's sons be hung up for public display. Three hundred more die the second day. Meanwhile, fighting in the provinces has left 75,000 enemies dead, a number as exaggerated as Ahasuerus's 180 days of partying, the virgins' twelve months of beauty treatments, and Haman's fifty-cubit-high stake. Although the decree had authorized plundering, three times it is said that the Jews do not touch the plunder.

Mordecai institutes the Jewish festival of Purim, or lots, to commemorate the event, because Haman cast lots to choose the day when the Jews would be destroyed. The chain of events is recapitulated, more is said about Purim, and then Queen Esther, along with Mordecai, sends another letter about Purim. The very short chapter 10 ends the book with further notes on the greatness of Ahasuerus and Mordecai.

The Feast of Purim

The Feast of Purim is a minor holiday and the most festive day on the Jewish calendar. Purim celebrates Mordecai and Esther's saving of the Jewish people from the massacre that Haman had planned. On Purim, the scroll of Esther is read in the synagogue, gifts of food are exchanged, charitable gifts are delivered, and a feast is prepared. During the reading of the scroll, participants twirl *graggers* (noisemakers) every time Haman's name is mentioned.

The Septuagint version follows the same outline but abbreviates some sections and differs in some details. The killing is deemphasized—only 15,000 people die, rather than 75,000. Haman's sons have different names. At one point the Jews take plunder, and at two points they do not. The book ends with a large section, Addition F, that does not exist in the Hebrew at all, in which Mordecai interprets an allegorical dream he had at the beginning of the story.

The ending in the A-Text is quite different from both of these, and considerably shorter. In this version, Haman's edict is *not* irrevocable, so Mordecai simply asks that it be revoked. Esther asks to punish her enemies with slaughter, and the king grants permission. Mordecai sends a letter explaining that Haman and his family are dead. Seven hundred are slain in Susa, and plunder is taken. In the rest of the kingdom, 70,100 die. Mordecai sends a decree instituting a holiday called Phourdaia on the fourteenth and fifteenth of Adar. No mention is made of a second day of battle or of a difference in dates for the cities and countryside, and very little is said about the customs of the holiday. The story is not recapitulated, and Esther sends out no letter. At the very end, Mordecai actually succeeds Ahasuerus as emperor of Persia.

The differences among these three versions resemble what happens to an anecdote when it is told and retold by various people who do not remember the details quite the same way. Though our job as readers would be easier without these complexities, the problem of different versions is not limited to Esther. It is central to biblical tradition, from the two stories of creation to the four stories of Jesus' resurrection. Which disciples went to the tomb, what happened when they got there, when and where and how Jesus appeared to people, what he said and did—each Gospel

> **Apocrypha**
>
> The Apocrypha is a group of books or parts of books that are not part of the Jewish canon but are found in early Christian versions of the Old Testament. The rest of the book of Esther, also called the Greek Book of Esther, is comprised of six additions to Esther that are not in the original Hebrew. These additions are placed in the Apocrypha in English-language Protestant Bibles but are included with the book of Esther in Roman Catholic Bibles.

tells these things differently. Christians have lived mostly untroubled by these distinct resurrection stories, since they agree on the most important points: that for Jesus, and for us, death is not the end of the story, and that God's power reaches beyond the grave.

Similarly, in all of Esther's endings, the roles are reversed between the Jews and their enemies, and those who seek to destroy the Jews are themselves destroyed. The powers of death are overturned, and the Jews celebrate gaining rest from their enemies. Like the parallel Gospel narratives, the three versions of Esther bring us face to face with the Bible's complex history of transmission and compilation. They remind us that the Bible did not simply fall from the sky sometime in the misty past in the King James Version. Rather, it was shaped by the theological and scribal genius of many generations of writers. Other biblical books, such as Genesis, Jeremiah, 1–2 Samuel, and 1–2 Chronicles, reveal their own complex origins in a variety of ways to readers attentive enough to note the seams in their fabric.

Esther's Response

Looking more closely at the Hebrew version of the story, readers differ distinctly in their reactions to the events of Adar. Issues often discussed are the character of Esther herself and the matter-of-fact reporting of massive carnage. While Esther's ending is admittedly ragged, it is helpful to think carefully about what the story is and is not.

Esther's confidence before the king has been on the move since the beginning of the book. Her first request took three conversations to articulate. Her reiteration of that request in chapter 8 came more forthrightly, though it too was prefaced by several deferential phrases. But by this final exchange, it seems the king and Esther have routinized the "what is your petition" drill. The king responds to the information about the carnage in Susa by wondering how many have been killed in the provinces, and by asking what Esther would like now. He seems more to be seeking advice than extending a privilege. If his words seem strangely philosophical, at least it can be noted that for once he is taking initiative.

Esther replies, "If it pleases the king, let the Jews who are in Susa be allowed tomorrow also to do according to this day's edict, and let the ten sons of Haman be hanged on the gallows" (9:13). This response strikes some as shockingly bloodthirsty for a young woman who was recently so reticent. Several observations can be made, however. First, her simple answer, prefaced by the brief, "If it pleases the king," completes the sequence of change in her confidence before the king. She can now state what she wants without excessive deference or delay. It is also noted that in a situation of great danger, both the Jews and Esther show remarkable restraint. The times, places, and subjects of retribution are carefully circumscribed in a way unheard of in real life, and are carried out only by the king's explicit authorization. Her request that Haman's sons be put on display, gritty as it is, can be viewed as a measure to horrify potential enemies into eschewing the battle. It might also be asked whether gender stereotypes play into readers' responses to Esther here: Would we dislike it as much if Mordecai had been the one to make these requests?

The second line of discussion about her response has to do with the description of Purim practices that follows. The story presents the second day of fighting in Susa as the reason Purim is celebrated on a different day in cities than in the countryside. Here it seems that history has followed practice, that is, a peculiarity in the dating of the custom may have inspired the story of a second day of fighting, rather than the other way around. Esther may need to ask this in order to make the custom make sense.

Why Have a Battle at All?

The fact that a happy ending in a biblical book should involve violence is disconcerting to modern people. Certainly this is no Quaker ending, and few would argue that the defensive battle is palatable. But it can well be asked what kind of ending is preferable.

If Haman had been the Jews' only real enemy, his death alone would have resolved the issue. Throughout the book it has never been clear how widespread hatred against the Jews is. Mordecai's precautions about Esther's secrecy concerning her lineage, the mentions of his Jewishness in 3:4 and 6:13, and Haman's confidence that his edict will be obeyed suggest that there is some cause for concern.

By the time of the thirteenth day of Adar, Haman has been dead several months, and "fear of the Jews had fallen upon" many people, some of whom had even professed to be Jews. Even so, thousands of enemies rise up to kill them according to Haman's decree. Why so many persist in battle when the tide has so decisively turned against them is puzzling. Especially puzzling is why, after the first day's rout in Susa, so many enemies show up for a futile battle on the second day.

For many readers, a more ideal ending to the story might have been a massive change of heart, rendering death unnecessary. But this is not a story in which such divine interventions prevail. What happens here has sometimes been compared with the fighting in the Warsaw ghetto during World War II, in which Jews being attacked by Nazis rose up to defend themselves. The fighting is certainly much more limited in scale and scope than the wars in U.S. history, none of which were limited to one or two days and some of which would be difficult to categorize as purely defensive.

47

A world in which enemies rise up to kill or be killed faces people of faith with extremely difficult questions. Is it right to kill in self-defense? What constitutes self-defense? At what cost is security attained? What is the cost to our families and to civilization of the refusal to defend one's community? These are questions hotly debated today even in the United States, the most powerful country in the world. If Americans in all our isolation feel so insecure, we must be careful to avoid hypocrisy in judging the situation in Esther's Persia.

As subjects of successive empires from Assyrian times on, Jews have long lived as minorities in a world where their safety perennially depended upon the policies of those in charge. Though the authors of Esther could not have known this, Jewish communities would be dispersed throughout the world for millennia to come. A recent publication of the Hadassah International Research Institute on Jewish Women at Brandeis University gathered descriptions of Purim celebrations from Jews in a staggering ninety-five countries throughout the world, from Ireland to Ecuador to Mali to Trinidad, in which Jews live today as minority populations.

Want to Know More?

About alternate endings to Esther? See Bechtel, *Esther*, 85–98.

About Purim? See Paul J. Achtemeier, ed., *HarperCollins Bible Dictionary*, rev. ed. (New York: HarperCollins, 1996), 901–2.

Jewish fortunes have risen and fallen with their favor with the particular rulers of particular times and places. It is to the shame of Western Christians that anti-Judaism has had its largest impact over the past thousand years in Christian Europe, culminating in the systematic slaughter of six million Jews during World War II. Over the centuries, especially in situations of great community danger, stories of deliverance have given Jews hope that ultimately they would be safe, as we all deserve to be. Even in the midst of cruelest oppression, stories like Esther, and the annual Purim celebration inspired by the story, have served to suggest that danger would not always be the way of life, that providential forces may yet redeem what is out of joint in the messy circumstances of life.

The battles at the end of Esther remind us that violence can be rooted in the desire for peace and security. Yet human experience teaches that peace is a precious, fleeting commodity, rarely won by escalated aggression. The Hamans of the world must be exposed and brought to justice. But how far must we go in order to limit the power of evil without violating the peace we are fighting for? This is an issue unresolved in both history and scripture.

Days of Celebration: Esther 9:20–10:3

The very last part of the book returns to the motif of banquets, but the last banquets are very different from the first. The first banquets celebrated the king's riches and occasioned violence against the queen and strictures against the women of the empire. This final celebration commemorates rest from violence and constraint. Purim occurs not on the day of the battle itself, as a celebration of victory, but on the following day, as a celebration of hard-won peace.

Several practices still followed on Purim are instituted in the final verses of Esther: There is feasting and celebration, and gifts are given to one another and to the poor. The central feature of Purim is a public reading of the scroll of Esther. Often the story is retold as a skit or play. Participants dress as characters in the story, enthusiastically clap and cheer for the story's protagonists, and sound noisemakers called *graggers* at the mention of Haman's name. Like Mardi Gras or Halloween, it is a day of raucous reveling. According to a long-standing rabbinic tradition, participants are authorized to drink until they cannot tell the difference between "blessed be Mordecai" and "cursed be Haman." Such a holiday, with emphasis on the reversal of power, the remembrance of the poor, and the inclusion of all, especially the children, stands at a great distance from the six months of reveling among the officers of the Persian empire and the forced viewing of the queen's beauty with which the story of Esther began.

The scope of Esther's story is colossal, radiating out as it

> "[Christians] would do well to remember, however, the main event of that celebration [Purim]: namely, the reading of the book of Esther. Surely, we can manage that much. Indeed, we should more than 'manage' it, because there is a sense in which this book may have come into our canon 'for just such a time as this' (4:14). It is a book, after all, about the struggle to be faithful in the midst of an increasingly unfaithful culture. . . . Yet, as the book itself reminds us in the story about Ahasuerus's sleepless night, a living word is no more than a dead letter if it is not read. Perhaps we should not wait for a sleepless night to read and preach and revel in the book of Esther."
> Bechtel, *Esther*, 83–84.

Purim gragger (noisemaker)

49

does to the 127 provinces of Persia, in its own day the world's greatest empire. Fortunately, for most of us, opportunities as dramatic as Queen Esther faced, calls to save all our people from utter destruction, are few and far between. But we all have plenty of opportunities to engage in smaller acts of courage and hope. The problem portrayed in the story of Esther, the problem of differences and divisions between people, is not likely to disappear in our lifetime. But like Esther, rather than remaining children, rather than ignoring what is overwhelming to us, each of us has the God-given grace within us to step forward on behalf of the people we care for, to engage in small acts of courage, even when we can hardly see what good they will do. And very often, when we do step forward, forces beyond our power will help us, as they helped Esther, in carrying out God's good purposes.

 ## Questions for Reflection

1. The author states that chapter 9 is "filled with inconsistencies and redundancies," leading some scholars to believe it was added at a later date. What do these inconsistencies and redundancies add to the story?

2. Does the violence that occurs in this chapter trouble you, given that some of it was requested by Esther? Why or why not? Would it have troubled you less if Mordecai had been the one who made the request? Why or why not?

3. The author writes that parts of this section "resemble what happens to an anecdote when it is told and retold by various people who do not remember the details quite the same way." Discuss a situation like this that has happened to you. What was the resolution?

4. Name some situations of violence or war in recent world history. In what cases do you believe the violence was justified, and in what cases do you believe it was excessive and/or unnecessary?

Naomi No More

The small sphere of most of our worlds, and the invitation to small acts of courage, brings us to the story of Ruth. Like Esther, Ruth is a woman in an alien land. Like Esther, she acts on behalf of family members, on the basis of principles, and without clear divine guidance. And as in Esther, the beauty of her story emerges from the confluence of human action and redeeming grace.

Like the book of Esther, Ruth begins outside of Israel, in exile. Whereas Esther's exile was the well-known national catastrophe of the Babylonian conquest, the exile with which Ruth begins stems from local, natural causes: A famine in Bethlehem (ironically, "house of bread") sends Elimelech and his family east to the neighboring country of Moab, a region in present-day Jordan.

The setting of Ruth's story is much earlier than that of Esther. Whereas Esther's events take place long after the time of the Davidic kings, when the Jews were ruled by the Persian empire, Ruth is set long before David, during the time when the land of Israel had been settled but was still being ruled by "judges," individuals who by dint of their leadership skills were considered rulers but who did not customarily establish dynasties.

> **Who Wrote the Book?**
>
> The authorship of the book of Ruth is uncertain. Jewish tradition attributed the book to the prophet Samuel. Some recent scholars, however, have raised the possibility that the book was written by a woman and passed on by a guild of women storytellers.

But the end of the book, with its reference to King David, indicates that the author and earliest audience lived at least several generations later. There is much debate over when and for what purpose Ruth was written. Some view the book as having been written to legitimize David's claim to the throne, and thus dating from the early centuries of the Judean monarchy. Most, however, on the basis of linguistic features as well as subject matter, view the book as having been written much later, after the end of the monarchy and during Babylonian or Persian times. Many view its effect, and perhaps even its purpose, as proposing a more inclusive view of Israelite society than that reflected in such books as Ezra and Nehemiah, a view in which foreigners are welcomed into the congregation of worshipers of Israel's God.

This is an important theme in Ruth. While the name Moab means little to most modern people, for ancient readers of Ruth it would have been freighted with meaning. This is not like a move from Michigan to Canada. Rather, it is a move to a place with a long history of close but difficult, often hostile, relations with Israel. The Moabites are presented in the Bible as descendents of Lot's incestuous relationship with one of his daughters (Gen. 19), as inhospitable enemies who tried to call down a curse on the wandering Israelites (Num. 22–24) and who succeeded in ensnaring some Israelites in

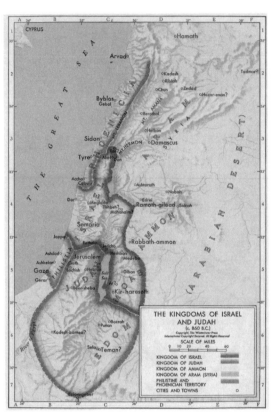

Map showing Moab and Judah, including Bethlehem

sexual sin (Num. 25). According to law, no Ammonite or Moabite was admitted to the worshiping assembly (Deut. 23:3). To early readers, Elimelech's choice to seek refuge in Moab would have seemed odd if not downright foolhardy, and his family's ill fortunes there completely unsurprising. Rather, surprise would have come later in the book, as a Moabite woman emerged as the story's heroine.

How Two Women Become a Pair: Ruth 1:1–7

The book opens by summarizing a tragic family history. To escape famine in Bethlehem, a couple and their two sons travel alone to a hostile land. Then the small family's future begins to perish. The husband Elimelech dies. Both sons take Moabite wives but, ten years later, catastrophically and improbably, both die childless. Three men and three women together have not managed to produce a single living heir. Not only has Bethlehem itself, the "house of bread," become fruitless, but this Bethlehemite family is on the verge of extinction. The household's survivors are the three women who married into the ill-fated family, three women from three different homes in two countries. Naomi, Orpah, and Ruth, three women who left their homes to cleave to husbands, are now a household of widows. The family's core has disappeared, or so it seems.

The paired relationships in this opening summary are worth noting. Naomi is first paired with Elimelech, and they have a pair of sons. Their little household is dominated by men. After Naomi loses her mate, she remains alone while the pair of sons take a pair of wives, swelling the household to five, and tipping the gender balance toward the women. Both sons die, and the pair of daughters-in-law sets out with Naomi to go to Bethlehem. Only when, after Naomi's first speech to her two daughters-in-law, one of them turns away does Naomi regain a "mate"—the unlikely younger, foreign woman Ruth. Naomi ends where she began, with a household of two. All that a husband and two sons have produced for Naomi is one Moabite daughter-in-law.

Part of the appeal of the book of Ruth is this woman-to-woman relationship. Though the ancient Israelite population presumably included as many women as men, the biblical stories disproportionately chronicle the names, deeds, and speech of men. Even when women appear, they generally appear in relation to men. As a result, conversations between women are extremely rare in the pages of the Bible, found only in a handful of passages: Genesis 30:14–15 (between Rachel and Leah, about Jacob); Exodus 2:7–9 (between Pharaoh's daughter and Moses' sister, and then his mother, about Moses); Mark 6:24 (between Herod's daughter and wife, about the head of John the Baptist); Luke 1:42–55 (between Elizabeth and Mary, about their unborn sons). In a handful of additional passages, one woman speaks to another but is not answered: Genesis 35:17

(midwife to dying Rachel, about her son); 1 Samuel 4:20 (midwife to dying wife of Ichabod, about her son); 2 Kings 5:3 (a servant girl to Naaman's wife, about Naaman); John 11:28 (Martha to Mary, about Jesus). In every single case, the topic of these conversations is a man.

> Outside of the book of Ruth, there are very few woman-to-woman conversations recorded in the Bible. These include Genesis 30:14–15 (between Rachel and Leah); Mark 6:24 (between Herod's daughter and wife); Luke 1:42–55 (between Elizabeth and Mary); and John 11:28 (between Martha and Mary). In all of these instances, the topic of the conversation is a man.

But the tiny book of Ruth devotes more verses to speech between women than the rest of the Bible combined: 29 verses encompassing eight dialogues. The first spoken words in the book are Naomi's to Ruth and Orpah (1:8–13), and the final words are those of the townswomen to Naomi (4:14–17). In between, five conversations occur between Ruth and Naomi alone (1:15–17; 2:2; 2:19–22; 3:1–5; 3:16–18), and one between Naomi and the townswomen (1:19–21). The dialogues between Ruth and Naomi stand out not only for their frequency but for their length, involving up to five speeches in succession. Most of all, they stand out for their subject matter: not only men but one another's welfare, the day's events, and food.

Thinking Inside and Outside the Box: Ruth 1:8–18

All the normal systems in the world of men have failed this family. Naomi is both displaced and bereft. Ruth and Orpah set out with her to return to Bethlehem, but after the journey has begun, she seems to have second thoughts. She informs her two foreign daughters-in-law that she has been thinking their predicament through. She urges them to leave this patchwork quilt of nonblood relationships and to return to traditional household patterns, to go home to their own mothers, in the hope that they might begin afresh, seeking their security and future with new husbands. Although it is men who have let these women down, Naomi continues to maintain that their redemption lies with men.

Ruth and Orpah are reluctant to break up their home of the past ten years. The men have left, but these two women will not leave. They give no reason for this wish, and do not even bother to argue with Naomi's logic. They simply refuse to leave. Death and departure have dominated this household's story, and they refuse to participate in further separation. Their future is with the one person who has not left them.

As she shows in the falsely logical verbal picture she draws for them next, Naomi persists in thinking "inside the box." She has nothing left to give them, she says. She has no sons left in her womb, and no husband to help produce them. And even if she had, they have no time to wait for such an improbable future. Although their marriages have hitherto produced only grief, Naomi still views security through marriage as their highest hope, and she has nothing left for them toward that end. It is bad enough that she faces an empty future; she cannot drag them into it as well.

The narrator expresses no criticism of Orpah for allowing Naomi's speech to persuade her. All we see of Orpah is her gesture of affection toward Naomi, kissing her; the narrator does not even describe her leaving. We find out she is gone only through Naomi's words.

For a third time Naomi speaks up. Now Elimelech, Mahlon, Chilion, and Orpah have all left the household, and Ruth alone remains. Naomi urges her once again to turn back as her sister-in-law has done.

The speeches of Naomi and Ruth's reply to her are a study in contrasts. Naomi's speech had descended from a parting blessing that disturbingly linked herself with the dead rather than the living ("May the LORD deal kindly with you, as you have dealt with the dead and with me," 1:8), to the balder claim of mistreatment at God's hands ("It has been far more bitter for me than for you, because the hand of the LORD has turned against me," 1:13), to the simple insistence that Ruth follow Orpah's example and leave. Her speeches are laden with bitter past and impossible future. They give in to abandonment by God and by humans, and attempt to persuade Ruth to do as everyone else has done to her. Naomi seems convinced that it is pointless to defy the relentless downturn of her fortunes. Ruth must save herself by leaving this God-forsaken household.

Ruth's well-known words to Naomi completely change the subject. Though she could well have inquired what good to a foreigner is a wish for kind dealings from an Israelite God who hasn't dealt kindly with Israelites, she avoids debating divine intentions. Though she could well have disputed the sense of continuing to pursue personal security when such pursuit has hitherto gained them nothing, she declines to argue over strategy. Unlike Naomi, she neither rehearses the past nor speculates on the future. She is not concerned with ends or means to ends. Rather than deserting Naomi to better her own chances for family and future, she pledges to do the one thing no one else has been able to do: to stay. Sticking closer than a shadow, she will mirror every one of Naomi's movements. She will go where Naomi goes, sleep where Naomi sleeps, claim Naomi's kindred and even her unkind God as Ruth's own. Then in the height of rhetorical audacity, Ruth adds one more promise. Whereas Elimelech, Mahlon, and Chilion had been forced by death to abandon them, Ruth pledges—as if she could carry it out—that not even death will come between them. Unlike Naomi's, her words are not about marriage, not about theology, not about strategy, but only about presence. She throws in her lot with the one who believes her fortune has completely run out.

> "For Naomi, Ruth's presence is as much a reminder of tragedy as it is a potential comfort. Naomi has no idea how she herself will be received upon returning to Bethlehem, and now she also has a foreign companion to be explained. . . . Is Ruth to be primarily a reminder of the past or will she become a source of hope for the future?"
> Sakenfeld, *Ruth*, 35.

Naomi's only reply is silence. What do we read into this silence? Is she pleased with Ruth's loyalty? Grieved to face this daily reminder of her lost husband and sons? Angry at being contradicted and thwarted? Longing to be free of foreigners? Humbled at Ruth's fierce fidelity? Disconcerted at the refusal of her wise counsel? Yearning for solitude to brood? Wary of entrusting her future to yet another mortal? Afraid to relax in the comfort of companionship? We do not know. We only know that "when Naomi saw that she was determined to go with her, she said no more to her" (1:18). Her opening words to her old friends in Bethlehem, declaring that God has brought her back empty (1:21), suggest that she is less than impressed by Ruth's devotion.

Three Different Theologies

Three different voices speak in chapter 1, expressing three different views of God. Naomi's theological discourse is quite extensive. In the course of her seven mentions of God, her speech becomes more and more embittered. At first she hopes God will reciprocate the Moabite women's kindness. Then she declares to Ruth and Orpah that God's hand has turned against her (1:13). Her complaints to the women of Bethlehem who welcome her are loud and long: "The Almighty has dealt bitterly with me . . . has brought me back empty . . . has dealt harshly with me . . . has brought calamity upon me" or, literally, "done evil to me" (1:20–21). Her speech has descended from the wish that God bless her daughter-in-law to the claim that God has done evil to her. Everything that has happened to her can be traced back to a harsh and devastating God.

The narrator has had very little to say directly about God's dealings, but the little that is there contrasts sharply with Naomi's viewpoint and subtly critiques it. Though Naomi fails to acknowledge God's responsibility for anything good, the narrator tells us that the reason she returns from Moab is that she heard that God had given food to her people again (1:6).

Ruth has even less theological comment than the narrator. What little she has to say focuses on her own, not God's, activities: "Your God [will be] my God" (1:16), she promises. When she expresses the wish that God "do thus and so to me, and more as well" (1:17), if death parts her from Naomi, she is invoking an ancient formula approximately equivalent to, "I'll be damned if . . ." Both of these statements may be taken as rhetorical flourish. But taken more seriously, on the heels of Naomi's bitter remarks, both of them suggest Ruth is boldly signing on to whatever treatment may be forthcoming from the God who Naomi claims is so cruel, and that she is more concerned with taking responsibility than with placing it.

Is Naomi Empty? Ruth 1:19–22

Naomi has not been forgotten in Bethlehem. The whole town notices her arrival. The women recognize her immediately, though they are a little unsure whether she is truly who they think she is. Naomi is no longer a stranger in a strange land but is back where there are people who recognize her and are moved by her arrival. Her response fails to acknowledge her suddenly changed status. Distancing herself from the name by which the whole town knows her, she denies being Naomi ("pleasant") anymore. Call her Mara ("bitter") instead, she says. "I went away full," she claims (1:21), though the narrator has already told us there was a

Want to Know More?

About the possibility that the book of Ruth was written by a woman? See Sakenfeld, *Ruth,* 5; Fokkelien van Dijk-Hemmes, "Ruth: A Product of Women's Culture?" in *A Feminist Companion to Ruth,* ed. A. Brenner (Sheffield: Sheffield Academic Press, 1993), 134–39.

About Moab and the Moabites? See Paul J. Achtemeier, ed., *HarperCollins Bible Dictionary,* rev. ed. (New York: HarperCollins, 1996), 691–92.

famine (1:1). "The LORD has brought me back empty" (1:21), she claims, though Ruth is standing by her side.

Though Naomi never acknowledges the one divine activity recounted in the book thus far, God's provision of food, the storyteller appends to this account a nearly parenthetical remark underscoring the truth of the rumor: She has arrived at the beginning of the barley harvest. After a whole chapter of fruitlessness, the last phrase whispers a hint of the upturn of Naomi's fortunes.

Kathleen Robertson Farmer, commenting on the book of Ruth, suggests Naomi as the character who "most closely mirrors the attitudes and experiences of the people of God, including both Israel and the church" (892), a character who is redeemed through the agency of another's actions. Like the parable of the good Samaritan, the story of Ruth calls attention to the merciful actions of foreigners, and convicts the "chosen" of our own failure to mirror divine hospitality. Neither the narrator nor any of the characters ever chides Naomi for her bitterness. Nor should we, unless we too have been exiles in a hostile land, bereft of our immediate family, and without Medicare or social security. The point here is not whether Naomi's attitude is faithful, but how God will freely shape out of the most unlikely ingredients a redemptive future not only for Naomi but for many others as well.

? Questions for Reflection

1. Read some or all of the following passages: Genesis 30:14–15; Exodus 2:7–9; Mark 6:24; Luke 1:42–55. In what ways are these conversations between women similar? In what ways are they different?

2. In her commentary on Ruth, Kathleen Farmer suggests that Naomi is the biblical character who "most closely mirrors the attitudes and experiences of the people of God." Do you agree? Why or why not?

3. Read Ruth's famous words to Naomi (1:16–17). Why is it significant that these words come from a woman from Moab?

4. What risks did Ruth take in leaving Moab? Can you think of similar risks that women must take today?

Reaping Redemption

Ruth's second chapter narrates a single day filled with events and speeches. The chapter begins and ends as the day does, with conversations at home between Ruth and Naomi. In between, Ruth's adventures away from home begin to turn the two women's fortunes around. The chapter's central portion occurs in the field of a kinsman of Naomi's named Boaz. Whereas in chapter 1, repeated disasters had embittered Naomi and created disagreement over the course the women should take, chapter 2 is increasingly overfilled with goodwill, good fortune, and well-being.

Juxtaposed Information: Ruth 2:1–2

The sequencing of information in the chapter's initial verses is worth noting. It was stated just previously (1:22) that Naomi and Ruth arrived in Bethlehem as the barley harvest began. It might be natural for 2:2 to follow immediately: "And Ruth the Moabite said to Naomi, 'Let me go to the field and glean among the ears of grain, behind someone in whose sight I may find favor.'" But before Ruth has a chance to speak, the narrator offers a bit of information that is not immediately connected, and in fact remains unacknowledged by the characters throughout most of the chapter. This information creates anticipation for the readers, who are positioned to know some things that each of the characters knows, and more than any one of them does.

What we are told in the first verse is that Naomi's husband Elimelech has a kinsman named Boaz, a "prominent rich man," or more literally, "a mighty man of strength" (*ish chail*), a phrase more often used of warriors than of landholders. Other English translations read "a man of wealth," "a man of substance," "a man of standing," "well-to-do." One translation, drawing from the fact that one of the pillars of the temple later was named Boaz (1 Kings 7:21), calls him "a pillar of the community." Immediately readers are tantalized over why Boaz has been introduced and what he will have to do with Naomi. We learn also, in verse 2, that Naomi is empty not only of family members but also of food, a factor that had not been discussed in chapter 1, though it is not surprising. We are introduced to the women's poverty only by hearing of Ruth's resourcefulness. Their need stands in immediate contrast to their kinsman's wealth.

Who Is Boaz?

There are many different English translations of the description of Boaz. These include: *a man of wealth, a man of substance, a man of standing, well-to-do, a prominent rich man, a mighty man of strength,* and *a pillar of the community.*

Ruth proposes to do what Israel's destitute were allowed by law to do, that is, to glean grain (see Lev. 19:9–10). Reading linearly, we may experience a repeated urge to connect Ruth's proposal with the information about Boaz. Yet it does not connect at all: "Let me go" (go and meet Boaz?) "Let me go to the field" (go and seek a job from Boaz?) "Let me go to the field and glean" (ah! glean in Boaz's field!) ". . . behind someone in whose sight I may find favor." We finally realize that Ruth knows nothing of Boaz. As far as she knows, their only resource is the kindness of strangers.

Ruth gleaning in the fields

Assuming that Naomi stands to benefit from this suggestion, and assuming that a woman capable of walking from Moab can walk through a field and pick up grain, or at least that she knows more about the customs and people of her hometown than Ruth does, we might expect from her a more helpful response than Ruth receives. In fact, cued in to the existence of a wealthy kinsman, and still wondering how he will enter the story, we might well expect Naomi to direct Ruth to Boaz's field. But Naomi manages no more helpful a reply than "Go, my daughter." Has she forgotten Boaz? Or is she too despondent to consider her resources? What would she have done had she been alone, had Ruth not insisted on coming with her and going out to seek food?

Coincidental Encounter: Ruth 2:3–7

Esther is not the only book laden with divine coincidence. When Ruth goes out, we are told that "as it happened, she came" (literally, "her chance chanced her") to Boaz's property. High coincidence is emphasized in this phrasing: No human agency caused this to happen. Moreover, the narrator says, here comes Boaz himself. As readers who have been cued in to all the players, we are aware long before Ruth is of her good fortune, and we are invited to savor its unfolding.

Boaz enters singing out divine blessings to his employees, who greet him in kind. Given that Naomi has already declared that God is not with her but against her, and has dealt her not blessing but evil, Boaz's assumption of God's generosity is striking.

Immediately he notices Ruth and inquires about her, asking not who she is but *whose* she is. What stands behind this phrasing is not readily apparent. The field is full of young men and women hired to harvest, and he may be assuming she is someone else's employee. Or he may be asking to whom she is related, since he does not recognize her. In small-town Bethlehem, strangers are certainly conspicuous. Ironically, we will later learn that he is asking more than he knows: She is in fact nobody's but her own, and she will insist on becoming his wife.

His foreman's response only minimally answers the question as posed. No family relationship is supplied at all. Rather, her foreignness is emphasized: She is the Moabite from Moab who came back with Naomi. But the foreman goes on to tell Boaz about Ruth's work ethic. She asked if she could glean, and she has been on her feet tirelessly all morning. She has evidently impressed the speaker.

Getting to Know Boaz: Ruth 2:8–13

Boaz initiates a conversation with Ruth herself, beginning a series of hospitable gestures. The first five things he says amount to five ways of asking her to do exactly what she had requested: (1) do not glean in another field; (2) do not pass on from here; (3) stick close to "my young women"; (4) keep your eyes on the field that they reap; and (5) follow them. The man is used to giving orders! He further informs her that he has commanded his young men not to touch her. Then he begins extending the workers' benefits to her by inviting her to drink their water.

Ruth wants to know why she as a foreigner has found such favor. In Boaz's straightforward answer we discover something new: He knows more about her than he has just been told. Having found out she is the Moabite, he has pieced together that she is Naomi's widowed daughter-in-law, the one whose kindness to Naomi is well known around town.

He goes on to retell her story in much more lofty terms than it was told to us before. The man who entered the field sounding like a psalm does not hesitate to imbue Ruth's journey with theological significance. Commentators have often noted that Boaz draws a parallel between Ruth and his own ancestor Abraham, who also journeyed from the east, when he says, "You left your father and mother and your native land and came to a people that you did not know before" (2:11; see Gen. 12:1). Just as God had promised great reward to Abraham (Gen. 15:1), so Boaz wishes upon Ruth a full reward from the God of Israel. He ends with a lovely metaphorical interpretation of Ruth's adoption of Naomi's faith, speaking of the God "under whose wings you have come for refuge" (2:12).

As eloquently as Naomi had drawn the picture of her pain at God's hands, just as eloquently does Boaz draw another picture, a redemptive storyline for this stranger Ruth. It is hard to tell as yet whether his cultured speech is simply a fancy way of saying, "Go in peace, be warmed and filled" (Jas. 2:16 RSV), or whether he has more help to offer this woman he so evidently admires. On the one hand, he fails to mention that he is family; on the other hand, he proceeds throughout the day to give her particular attention and help—all, of course, with great propriety, as befits a pillar of the community.

In fact, although Boaz stands in contrast with Naomi financially, the two of them have quite a bit in common, signaled by their having both adopted the affectionate title "my daughter" for Ruth—a title that will be found on both their lips increasingly as the story progresses. This address, so frequent in this story, is found only once outside of Ruth, and then by an actual parent (Judg. 11:35). In addition to this shared title for Ruth, Boaz and Naomi both speak freely of God; both speak in rather stately, measured, archaic sentences, and both seem used to giving orders. They will both express concern for Ruth's physical safety. Despite all these similarities, and despite their kinship, they never meet in the course of the story, for Naomi remains in the inner world of her home, and Boaz moves around outdoors, in the field, at the threshing floor, and at the city gate.

Ruth is not at all daunted by Boaz's heaped-up phrases. She had set out to glean behind someone "in whose sight I may find favor," and twice she mentions this concept to Boaz. "Why have I found favor in your sight?" she asks. Then, even after he has explained what he knows and thinks of her, she requests once again to find favor in his eyes, because he has spoken kindly to her. She

Want to Know More?

About the role of the *go'el* (redeemer)? See Paul J. Achtemeier, ed., *HarperCollins Bible Dictionary*, rev. ed. (New York: HarperCollins, 1996), 919.

About farming and Levitical law? See Paul J. Achtemeier, ed., *HarperCollins Bible Dictionary*, rev. ed. (New York: HarperCollins, 1996), 331–32.

refers to herself as "your servant, even though I am not one of your servants" (2:13). She may mean she isn't *even* a servant but a mere foreigner, but as readers who know what she does not, we realize she has spoken correctly. She is certainly not a servant. She is family!

It is possible to read Ruth's polite words as expressions of humility. At the same time, she is in no hurry to conclude this conversation. She points out his notice of her and his effect upon her. Although there is nothing at all improper about his bearing toward her, his immediate and frequent arrangements for her welfare, coupled with his frequent warnings concerning the young men, tease us with the hint that his interest is not exclusively paternal. And while she does not flirt, she certainly does what she can to stay front and center in his eyes.

Seeds of Hope: Ruth 2:13–20

When the workers sit down to eat, Boaz beckons Ruth to join them, and gives her far more than she can eat. After the meal, he directs his laborers to leave more for her to glean, and even to pull out and leave stalks they have already cut. He is so generous, and she so industrious, that she heads home in the evening with an *ephah* of barley, that is, about forty-two quarts—quite a load to carry home after a day of backbreaking work.

This chapter uses several different words for what amounts to seeds of grain: "ears of grain" (2:2); "sheaves" (2:7, 15); "bread," "morsel," and "parched grain" (all in 2:14); "barley" (2:17, 23); and "wheat" (2:23). Boaz gives Ruth seed of many varied descriptions. Although the pun is never used directly in Ruth, the Hebrew word for "seed" is elsewhere used not only of grain but of human offspring and the semen that produces them. (See, for instance, in the King James Version, "seed" in Gen. 12:7 and in Lev. 15:16). Naomi's problem is the lack of seed of every kind: lack of grain, lack of offspring, and lack of the means of producing offspring. Boaz's generosity toward Ruth in the giving of so many kinds of grain, described in so many ways, foreshadows his later role as giver of human seed.

Ruth's conversation with Naomi at home that evening reveals the older woman's first glimmer of hope. Receiving both the gleaned barley and the leftovers from Ruth's meal, Naomi asks where Ruth worked, already breathing a blessing for whoever took notice of her. The narrator goes over Ruth's response twice, as if to savor the moment: "So she told her mother-in-law with whom she had worked, and said, 'The name of the man with whom I worked today is Boaz'" (2:19). Finally all the dots are connected, as Naomi first exclaims a second blessing for Boaz and then in a dramatic speech revises her earlier evaluation of God: Earlier God had been the one who had turned against her, dealt bitterly with her, and done evil to her (1:13, 20, 21), but now God is the one whose kindness has not forsaken the living or the dead after all.

> "Every generation of Jews and Christians has struggled with the meaning of personal calamity. Every faithful person at some time has reason to ask, 'why does it hurt so much?' Not all would agree with Naomi's assessment that God was the cause of her sorrow. Yet almost more important than assessing the cause is the realization that God does not abandon us in our suffering."
> Sakenfeld, *Ruth*, 48.

In saying this, Naomi happily repositions herself. Before, she had blessed her daughters-in-law for their kind dealings "with the dead and with me," as if she were counting herself nearly among the dead. But here she draws a distinction between the living and the dead, suggesting that perhaps she may once again count herself among the living. In addition, by using the same word that Ruth used when refusing in chapter 1 to abandon Naomi (1:16, translated as "leave" in the NRSV), she draws a verbal connection between Ruth's action and that of God who, it turns out, has not abandoned her after all (2:20, translated as "forsaken" in the NRSV).

Boaz the Redeemer: Ruth 2:21–23

Naomi informs Ruth that Boaz is one of "our" nearest kin, now including Ruth in the family circle. She also introduces a word that will become extremely important throughout the rest of the book. The word translated in the NRSV variously as "kinsman," "near kinsman," and "next-of-kin," and in the NIV as "kinsman-redeemer," is the Hebrew word *go'el*. This word designates one who buys a relative's property in order to keep it in the family (see, for example, Lev. 25:25), or who buys a relative out of slavery (see, for example, Lev. 25:48). The redeemer is also the one who avenges a murder (Num. 35:19). By extension, God was called the one who redeemed Israel out of Egypt (Exod. 6:6) and who would redeem Israel from exile (Mic. 4:10). The idea of God's redemption of Judah from Babylon became a dominant metaphor of the exilic prophet in Isaiah 40–55. By further extension, the early church came to understand the concept of redemption primarily in terms of deliverance from bondage to sin (Col. 1:14). Though the term "redeemer" in Ruth is a familial and economic one, its theological dimensions should not be lost on us. Divine concern for the poor, the widows, and the foreigners is a dominant theme of Scripture, and in the story of Ruth, the redemption of these two women from their destitute condition has theological as well as economic significance.

Ruth has not finished announcing all that Boaz said. She reports that she has a place in his field throughout the harvest. When she erroneously says that Boaz told her to stay close to the young men (2:21, obscured in the NRSV by the gender-neutral term "servants"; see Boaz's words in 2:8: "Keep close to my young women"), Naomi corrects her, suggesting that she go out with the young women for her own safety (2:22). That is what Ruth does every day until the end of the barley harvest and the end of the wheat harvest, about seven weeks.

? Questions for Reflection

1. Why do you think Naomi stayed away from the fields, sending Ruth instead?

2. Why didn't Boaz reveal his relationship to Naomi when he first met Ruth?

3. What do you make of Boaz's extremely generous treatment of Ruth? Was it because she was kin? Because he was interested in her? Because he was a "redeemer"?

4. Note Naomi's reversal of her earlier judgment against God (1:13, 20, 21) in this chapter. Has there been a time in your life when your anger at God has suddenly given way to great joy?

9

Winnowing, Wings, and Weddings

The second chapter of Ruth related the events of a single day, beginning and ending with conversations between Ruth and her mother-in-law at home. These domestic conversations formed bookends around Ruth's interactions with Boaz in his field. The third chapter likewise begins and ends with conversations between Ruth and Naomi at home. As in chapter 2, this chapter's center relates an encounter between Ruth and Boaz away from home. But whereas the previous events happened in public in the course of a day, chapter 3's events happen in secret in the course of a night. Both times, Boaz sends Ruth home loaded down with grain. The events of chapter 2 mark the beginning of Ruth's career as a scavenger of food for herself and Naomi; the events of chapter 3 ensure the ending of that stopgap measure, just when the harvest is complete and the potential for gleaning has passed.

Naomi's Proposal: Ruth 3:1–4

Chapter 2 began with Ruth's resourceful plan. Now it is the newly hopeful Naomi who unfolds a resourceful, if morally audacious, plan. She poses her idea in terms of the concern she first voiced in chapter 1: ensuring a secure home and future (literally, "resting place") for her daughter-in-law. Once Naomi urged Ruth to return to her mother's family because she had no further security to provide. Now Naomi sees a way her own family can help.

Rather than spelling out her goal, Naomi leaves it to Ruth's imagination and ours. What she makes explicit are her instructions, instructions that must have seemed odd indeed: Since Boaz is winnowing grain this evening, take a bath! Naomi instructs Ruth to look and smell sweet—not an easy task in the days before indoor plumbing, washing machines, and antiperspirant. After bathing, anointing herself, and dressing, she is to go stealthily to Boaz's threshing floor. When he is alone, full of wine and food, and lying down to sleep, she is to go lie down with him, and do whatever he says.

Needless to say, Naomi's instructions to Ruth have not been passed down through the ages as a model of dating protocol for young women of faith. Whereas in chapter 2 Naomi showed careful concern for Ruth's physical safety in a field full of young men, what she is suggesting here is that Ruth deliberately place herself in a more precarious spot than she could have ever encountered there. Ruth is to travel alone at night, make herself sexually available to a man who has been drinking, and then do whatever he says.

Sexual overtone is inescapable in her vocabulary. Not only is the Hebrew word for "lie" (used three times in verse 4) often used in the sexual sense of "lie with," not only is "uncover" often used in phrases referring to sex, but even the word innocuously translated as "feet" is related to a common biblical euphemism for genitals. All of these words will be repeated again as the narrator describes Ruth's actions. As Sakenfeld comments, "Never is there any indication of the consummation of sexual relations, yet the choice of words keeps that possibility always before the reader" (54).

"Needless to say, Naomi's instructions to Ruth have not been passed down through the ages as a model of dating protocol for young women of faith."

Why does Naomi propose this method of getting his attention? Why doesn't she talk to him herself? The answer is not clear. Perhaps Naomi's reasoning lies precisely with Boaz's apparent reticence. Perhaps she feels he needs the push of sexual possibility to jump-start his initiative.

Ruth's Improvements: Ruth 3:5–9

A protest from Ruth, or at least a request for further clarification, might have been in order. No matter what readers might wonder about this plan, Ruth simply agrees: "All that you tell me I will do," she says (v. 5). However, we will do well to pay careful attention to who ends up doing what who says in the action that follows.

Ruth begins exactly as Naomi told her. After Boaz eats and drinks, he lies down at the corner of the pile of grain. (Note once again the abundance and proximity of "seed.") She uncovers his feet and lies down—and nothing happens! Apparently, the man is already dead to the world.

Halfway through the night he awakens, startled to find a woman lying at his feet. What an odd predicament for a pillar of the community! How many times had this honorable man ever woken up with a woman in his bed and no recollection of how she got there? As Sakenfeld notes, his question, "Who are you?" may have con-

Ruth and Boaz

veyed "surprise, uneasiness, perhaps fear and even anger" (57).

His question forces Ruth to improvise. Contrary to Naomi's plan, he has not told her what to do at all. She answers his question as hastily as possible, emphasizing her connection not to her homeland nor to her mother-in-law but to him: "I am Ruth, your servant." Then (unlike a servant, and contrary to Naomi's instructions), she lets him know both what she is doing there and what she wishes: "Spread your wing over your maidservant because you are a redeemer" (3:9, author's translation).

Modern translations usually render the Hebrew word for "wing" as "cloak," "skirt," or "garment." Certainly part of the significance of her speech is this suggestion of sharing his cover. But more is going on here than those translations reveal. Ruth employs the same noun that Boaz had used in 2:12, when he described Ruth as having taken

69

refuge under the "wing" of the God of Israel. In response to Boaz's lofty description, Ruth had at that time hinted, by expressing the wish to find favor with him, that Boaz put his money where his mouth was. Here she is more direct. In saying "spread your wing," Ruth takes the action her mother-in-law directed her to do and imbues it with metaphorical meaning, turning Boaz's own words back on him, as if to say, "I have sought refuge under God's wing right here—under your wing. So spread your wing over me." She calls upon Boaz not merely to wish her well, not merely to greet her need with a congenial admonition to "be warmed and filled." She challenges him personally to provide, to embody, the divine refuge he had wished upon her. Just as Ruth had herself become the divine blessing standing between Naomi and emptiness, now she too invokes the intimate relationship between divine will and human action—that is, Boaz's action as kinsman and redeemer—on her own behalf.

> "Never is there any indication of the consummation of sexual relations, yet the choice of words keeps that possibility always before the reader." Sakenfeld, *Ruth*, 54.

Ruth brings up a topic that Boaz has not acknowledged before but that she knows about from Naomi: He is a "redeemer." As was mentioned in unit 7, a redeemer in the social world of ancient Judah was a relative who bore responsibility for care of kin in a variety of ways, reclaiming property or people sold for debts (Lev. 25:25, 48), or avenging a premeditated murder (Num. 35:19). Since there is no biblical record of the role of redeemer extending to marriage, there has been quite a bit of debate about what exactly Ruth is asking Boaz to do, and on what basis. Some see in her request the custom of levirate marriage (Deut. 25:5–10), in which a widow marries her brother-in-law to perpetuate her dead husband's lineage. Others point out that the primary concern voiced repeatedly by Naomi is not the death of the family name but Ruth's economic security.

The social law as outlined in the Pentateuch is suggestive rather than comprehensive, and it is clear that the common thread running through all functions of the "redeemer" is the provision of a safety net for family members who have fallen on hard times. Ruth's marital proposal seems to follow the lines of this more general function: By marrying her, Boaz will redeem her and her mother-in-law from their social and economic vulnerability brought about by famine, widowhood, and childlessness, compounded by a social structure that circumscribed opportunities for women and foreigners.

Boaz's Further Improvements: Ruth 3:10–15

As startled as Boaz was to find Ruth there, as soon as she identifies herself and makes her request, he shifts gears. The contents of his four-verse-long speech are rather remarkable and merit examination piece by piece:

First Boaz invokes a divine blessing upon her because he says, "this last instance of your loyalty is better than the first; you have not gone after young men, whether poor or rich" (v. 10). What is the first instance of her loyalty, and what is this last? The first seems to be what Boaz pointed out before, namely, Ruth's loyalty in accompanying Naomi to Bethlehem. The last is less clear. At first glance it may seem he is thanking her for taking interest in him rather than in a younger man. But why should he expect loyalty from her? He is more likely noting that she was under no familial obligation to marry within Naomi's clan, but in choosing Boaz for a husband she is assuring Naomi's future, and the future of Elimelech's lineage, as well as her own security.

Boaz continues: "And now, my daughter, do not be afraid, I will do for you all that you ask, for all the assembly of my people know that you are a worthy woman" (v. 11). A mouthful is said here. First, he acknowledges the precarious position in which she has placed herself and pledges to keep her from harm. Then he promises to do all that Ruth has asked. There is a subtle ironic twist to the question of who makes the request and who carries it out that bears delightful similarity to King Ahasuerus's repeated promise to Esther to give her whatever her request is. Earlier in the chapter, Naomi had told Ruth that Boaz would tell her what to do, and Ruth had responded that she would do what Naomi told her. But now that Ruth has taken the initiative, it is Boaz who pledges to do as she has asked.

The conclusion of this sentence, his comment about her worth, stands full in the face of any possible misconstrual of her actions: Far from the worthless woman who sneaks into men's beds uninvited, she is an *eshet chail,* a "worthy woman," according to the NRSV, or, to translate the Hebrew literally, a "woman of strength." He asserts that the whole community knows this about her.

His words here are highly significant in several ways. First, he has reassured her that her actions have inspired him to think more of her, not less. For a person as scrupulous as Boaz to make this assertion in the midst of a very compromising situation is remarkable. Second, he himself was introduced at the beginning of chapter 2 with an elaborated masculine form of the same phrase: "mighty man of strength" *(ish gibbor chail)*. The context of his landownership at that point suggested not only moral standing but economic substance. His use of this phrase to describe Ruth, in Sakenfeld's words, "collapses the social distance between them" (62). Third, his reference to Ruth as an *eshet chail* calls to mind the only other use of that phrase in the Bible, in Proverbs 31:10, which introduces an elaborate description of the qualities desired in a wife: "A woman of strength [*eshet chail,* often weakly translated as "capable wife" or "virtuous woman"] who can find?"

The first part of Boaz's speech is fully reassuring, and might lead swiftly to the conclusion of Ruth's story were it not for the new complication he now introduces, a complication that might help explain his previous reticence: "But now, though it is true that I am a near kinsman [redeemer], there is another kinsman [redeemer] more closely related than I" (v. 12). The story never spells out Boaz's precise familial relationship to Elimelech, nor that of this other relative. Why Boaz is obligated to defer to this other person is not clear, nor is it clear why Boaz first pledged to do as Ruth asked and then recalled this complication. Clearly one way or another Ruth and Naomi will be provided for, and he will make sure of it. But since neither we nor Ruth have met this other person, and since we have been rooting for Ruth and Boaz ever since their mutual admiration was expressed in the field, this complication introduces new suspense to a story that would have otherwise swiftly reached its conclusion. As Kirsten Nielsen notes, this delay not only makes a good story, it is also theologically significant, conveying that "God acts in spite of the hardships that arise, be they hunger, childlessness, or local custom" (78).

"Remain this night, and in the morning, if he will act as [redeemer] for you, good; let him do it. If he is not willing to act as [redeemer] for you, then, as the LORD lives, I will act as [redeemer] for you. Lie down until the morning" (3:13). Poignancy is suggested here. In a gesture that communicates both concern for Ruth's safety and desire to prolong this secret encounter, Boaz twice asks Ruth to stay. Is this the first of a lifetime of nights together, or are these their final hours before she marries a stranger? Only the morning will tell. Perhaps the path to the story's resolution will not be as straight as it initially appeared, but the complication is not one of discord but of scrupulous honor.

In the eerie half-light of dawn, Boaz sends Ruth home. Before she goes, Boaz once again gives her grain, a gesture that both reminds us of the weeks of labor in his field and foreshadows the "seed" he will give her at the story's conclusion. He himself loads the grain on her back, and they go their separate ways.

Ruth's Further Improvements: Ruth 3:16–18

Naomi has been eagerly awaiting the news of the night, and Ruth fills her in, supplying a speech for Boaz that he may or may not have actually said, a speech that includes Naomi in his circle of generosity: "Do not go back to your mother-in-law empty-handed"—or literally, "empty," the same term by which Naomi had described herself in her own return to Bethlehem, claiming that she went away full, but God brought her back empty (1:21). With Ruth around, Naomi has never been empty, and her arms will be even fuller soon.

> "God works throughout the biblical account, and throughout our own histories, to redeem the ones broken, disgraced, ignored, or harmed."

The two women's future is now assured, but what it will actually be hangs in the balance of the coming day's events. Naomi's enjoinder to wait to see how things turn out underlines for both Ruth and us that they are far from settled.

Ruth's actions of the night have danced on the edge of traditional moral virtue. Though Boaz interpreted them as a show of loyalty, they would have invited even more scandal in ancient Judah than in the most conservative of social settings today. Readers who maintain that the Bible unflaggingly upholds our conceptions of virtue, or that the biblical God dispenses reward and punishment in a wooden way, have not read scripture very closely. It is very much worth noting that the only biblical reference to Ruth outside of this book is in Matthew's genealogy of Jesus (1:5),

> The only reference to Ruth outside of this book is in Matthew's genealogy of Jesus (1:5), where among all the men only four women are listed: Tamar (Gen. 38), Rahab (Josh. 2), Ruth, and Bathsheba (2 Sam. 11–12).

where among all the men only four female ancestors are listed: Tamar, who tricked her own father-in-law into paternity (Gen. 38); Rahab the Canaanite prostitute, who betrayed her city to the Israelites (Josh. 2); Ruth; and Bathsheba, the wife of Uriah who bore David's son (2 Sam. 11–12). This litany of sexually irregular women leads up to the story of Mary's embarrassing pregnancy and the angel's instructions to Joseph to marry her anyway. Clearly Boaz is not this story's only redeemer. God works throughout the biblical account, and throughout our own histories, to redeem the ones broken, disgraced, ignored, or harmed.

? Questions for Reflection

1. Why do you think Naomi chooses to send Ruth to Boaz rather than going to speak to him herself?
2. Why does Ruth go along with Naomi's plan?
3. Like Esther, Ruth puts her safety and reputation on the line before a man of power in order to help others. What does this tell us about how God wants us to act toward our fellow humans?
4. In Matthew's genealogy of Jesus (1:5), only four female ancestors are listed: Tamar (Gen. 38), Rahab (Josh. 2), Ruth, and Bathsheba (2 Sam. 11–12). Discuss these women and what their inclusion in the genealogy tells us about redemption.

Bartering for the Bride

While chapters 2 and 3 of Ruth mirrored each other's actions, Ruth 4 serves to redeem the harm done to Elimelech's family in the book's opening. Just as the book began with a short listing of names and family history, the book ends with names and family history, creating an envelope around the action of the story. But whereas the opening genealogy led to dead ends, the closing genealogy will lead not only to life and continuation but straight into the most prominent family of ancient Judah, the lineage of King David's four-hundred-year-long dynasty.

In chapter 1, two women discussed marriage, children, and economics; in chapter 4, two men do so. The chorus of women who first listened to Naomi's complaints against God in chapter 1 will close the story by specifying the blessings God has given her through Ruth. Whereas Naomi had claimed, despite Ruth's company, to be empty, the townswomen remind her, even after her grandson is born, that Ruth herself was worth more than seven sons. In the end, all that was off-kilter is redeemed through human and divine loyalty.

Boaz Sets the Stage: Ruth 4:1–2

As Naomi predicted, Boaz sets out immediately to settle the matter. While his timing shows urgency, his leisurely pace suggests patient control of strategy and outcome. He does not simply knock on the other man's door and lay out the marriage question. Instead, he creates a very public, very formal, and very complex interaction. In chapter 3, Ruth had pledged to do what Naomi asked her, and had followed the spirit of her instructions while improvising to improve on the letter. Similarly, Boaz, who has pledged to do what Ruth asked, devises a circuitous route to comply with the spirit of Ruth's request. While Ruth carried out Naomi's scheme in secrecy at night, Boaz carries out Ruth's scheme publicly in broad daylight.

Stationing himself at the city gate during "rush hour," Boaz immediately finds the man he wants passing by. He bids him to turn aside and sit down and, reinforcing the effectiveness of Boaz's request, the man turns aside and sits down. His name is strikingly omitted. According to the NRSV and the NIV, he is called "friend," but in the Hebrew he is called *ploni almoni*, which roughly means "what's his name" or "so-and-so," indicating that Boaz called him by name but the narrator does not consider his name worth mentioning. From this point on, the narrator calls him *go'el*, "redeemer," with some irony since he will not turn out to be the redeemer after all. Even Orpah, who declined Ruth's role, was given a name, but this relative will decline Boaz's role and leave the stage anonymously.

> "By their actions, Ruth and Boaz give us a glimpse not just of how we should live, but also of what the loyal kindness of God might be like. . . . The story of Ruth and the story of Jesus Christ invite us to love loyal kindness and to follow the God in whom dividing walls of hostility are still being broken down." Sakenfeld, *Ruth*, 88.

Boaz assembles ten elders to act as witnesses to the conversation, and bids them likewise to sit down, and they do. What follows, with its explicit discussion of the buying of land and women, may seem on the surface like the "good old boy" network functioning in all its glory. However, Boaz uses the patriarchal customs not for exclusion and personal gain but for the inclusion of a foreign widow into the community, and for her and her elderly mother-in-law's enrichment. Boaz reminds us that virtue is found not in the acquisition or relinquishment of power in itself but in how and for whom it is used.

Boaz Sets the Trap: Ruth 4:3–4

The conversation itself is highly complex. Though its outcome is clear, exactly what is happening to get there is, for a number of reasons, somewhat less than clear. Readers with a legal or literary bent may enjoy perusing two or three commentaries that outline the questions and possibilities raised, such as those by Sakenfeld, Nielson, or Farmer. Only some aspects will be explored here.

Boaz begins by introducing a new piece of information, which is neither confirmed nor denied by the narrator: Naomi is selling a piece of land that was her husband's. Immediately several questions come to mind: What land? If she owned land, why was she hungry and empty? Why hasn't this been mentioned before? How does Boaz know this, and by what authority does he act? And what does all this have to do with Ruth? The only hint we are given in answer to these questions is the outcome of the conversation itself.

Boaz explains that he is giving "so-and-so" the opportunity to buy this land first, before Boaz himself does. Here we see a much more recognizable function of the "redeemer" at work. According to Leviticus 25:25, " If anyone of your kin falls into difficulty and sells a piece of property, then the next of kin shall come and redeem what the relative has sold." This was done to keep land within the family. Jeremiah 32:6–15 narrates an instance of this situation, in which Jeremiah redeems a piece of property from his cousin in the presence of witnesses.

Since Boaz makes it clear that he will buy the property if the other man will not, the other man is under no constraint. If Naomi had any male heirs, this purchase would not be advantageous for the relative, because sooner or later, when the year of Jubilee rolled around, the property would revert to her heirs and the relative would lose his investment. But if she has no heirs, he will be able "to do well by doing good," that is, to give her cash and acquire potentially valuable property for himself. Immediately he agrees to buy. Suddenly we realize that not only is this man the first who should have been helping her, but he also has the liquid assets to do so. Whether or not the property actually exists, Boaz has smoked out the family resources and motivations.

> **Jubilee**
>
> Jubilee was the year in which all land was returned to its ancestral owners and all Israelite slaves were freed. It happened at the end of seven Sabbatical cycles of seven years each, and was proclaimed by the blowing of the shophar (trumpet made from a ram's horn) on the Day of Atonement. The land was also left fallow in the Jubilee year.
>
> From Paul J. Achtemeier, ed., *Harper-Collins Bible Dictionary*, rev. ed. (New York: HarperCollins, 1996), 549.

Boaz Springs the Trap: Ruth 4:5–8

What Boaz says next is somewhat difficult to follow on account of a subtle but significant disagreement among ancient manuscripts. The two textual alternatives, differing only by the presence or absence of a single letter, create two different scenarios, both of them complex and interesting. According to the text followed by most modern translations, Boaz says, "The day you acquire the field from the hand of Naomi, you are also acquiring Ruth the Moabite, the widow of the dead man, to maintain the dead man's name on his inheritance" (4:5 NRSV). In other words, according to this reading, if so-and-so is going to help himself by redeeming the property, he also has an obligation to fulfill the role of "levir" to Ruth, marrying her to produce an heir for her dead husband—an heir who will inherit this property! (See p. 70 concerning levirate marriage, and the parallel wording in Deut. 25.) Since this revelation seems to come as a surprise to the poor man, we may assume that the obligation is more moral than legal. Yet by refusing the entire package, he acknowledges its validity.

But the Hebrew text itself, followed by some modern commentators, says something quite different: "The day you acquire the field . . . *I* [not "you"] will acquire Ruth. . . ." According to this reading, Boaz announces to the man Boaz's own intention to marry Ruth and produce a child who will inherit the property the man has just agreed to buy. If this is the case, who would marry Ruth was never in question. Rather, Boaz has added to Ruth's marriage proposal the task of reclaiming property that Naomi owned but had most likely lost use of during her ten-year absence. Some commentators even suggest that so-and-so, as next of kin, may have been farming the land. So-and-so is perfectly free to buy it from her outright now, but if Ruth has a child, so-and-so will permanently lose both the land and what he paid for it.

Either way, Boaz has cleverly and congenially set a trap for poor so-and-so, for whom the value of this investment has suddenly plummeted. Awkwardly he backs out of the deal, telling Boaz to acquire the property for himself, and in so doing, affirming the legitimacy of Boaz's application of law and custom.

Sexual economics play an interesting role in this transaction. It has already been noted that Naomi communicated several times in chapter 1 her expectation that men were needed for women's security. From the viewpoint of Ruth and especially of Naomi, Boaz is known as "the man" (see 2:19, 20; 3:3, 18; and also 3:8 and 16, where the narrator adopts the term from their speech). On one level, Boaz's significance to them is his patriarchal function as owner and sponsor. Perhaps in a corresponding way, Boaz's references to Ruth in his public conversation place her in a utilitarian role that makes modern readers squirm. He intends to acquire her as he acquires property. Her purpose is to produce babies for a dead man's lineage.

Yet on another level, as we have seen in Boaz's pledges to Ruth and their mutual interpretations of each other's generosity, more respect is operative than these functional roles suggest. Boaz does not view Ruth as mere property, nor does she view him merely as a meal ticket. In this transaction, to refer to her in terms of her personal value as *eshet chail* would endanger her request. In empha- sizing the redeemer's obligations and his own intentions, Boaz utilizes the crassest and most distancing language possible: "acquire Ruth the Moabite . . .

> "Boaz does not view Ruth as mere property, nor does she view him merely as a meal ticket."

widow . . . maintain . . . inheritance." This use is strategic: It disguises her worth, her participation, and his interest in her, reducing the competition he might otherwise encounter.

The Chorus Sings and the Curtain Rings: Ruth 4:9–22

Without further ado, Boaz turns to the elders he had called to oversee the conversation, declaring them witnesses that he is buying everything that belonged to Naomi and her dead family, including Ruth. He reit- erates the altruistic purpose of maintaining the name of the dead over the family property. Everyone present says as a chorus, "We are wit- nesses." They then pronounce a blessing upon Ruth that is filled with ironic significance. They invoke tradition, but the traditions invoked are highly selective. First they say, may God make her like Rachel and Leah—the two sisters by whose collective machinations the entire nation of Israel was born. Second they say, may your house become like that of the house of Perez—the son of Judah through his unintended levirate union with Tamar, who tricked him into giving her twins.

As soon as this elaborate transaction closes, in a single verse, Boaz and Ruth are wedded, bedded, and blessed with a son for whose con- ception God is given credit. This is only the second time in the book that the narrator attributes an action to God, the first being the gift of food in Ruth 1:6. The chorus of women who first appeared in chapter 1 to welcome Naomi home now interpret the story to her: God has given her a redeemer, who will be a "restorer of life and a nourisher of your old age" (4:15). Most significantly, they assert

Ruth and Naomi

Ruth's value to Naomi: "for your daughter-in-law who loves you, who is more to you than seven sons, has borne him" (4:15). In the end, after all this talk about husbands and sons, it is Ruth, the foreign widow who exercised exemplary loyalty to a bitter old woman, whose love and value are publicly extolled. As further signs of communal participation, Naomi takes the baby in her old arms, and her neighbors name him Obed.

The final genealogies serve as a punchline at the end of the story. The book of Esther had begun with the emperor of the known world and all his officers. By contrast, Ruth's beginning was very local, with an obscure, displaced, and bereft family of women. Ironically, the events of this story, we find out in the end, lead to an empire. While David's empire was never as far-flung geographically as Ahasuerus's, nor as famous in its own day, in subsequent human history it is arguably the more important one, living on as it does in the imagination and memory of both Jews and Christian throughout the world.

> "Together, the stories of Esther and Ruth, with their turning points in the loyal actions of obscure people, and especially young women, underscore the far-flung significance of small acts of courage, Ruth's on behalf of a family, and Esther's on behalf of a nation."

Together, the stories of Esther and Ruth, with their turning points in the loyal actions of obscure people, and especially young women, underscore the far-flung significance of small acts of courage, Ruth's on behalf of a family, and Esther's on behalf of a nation. Like Esther and Ruth and the people around them, no one knows for sure the providential possibilities that will be born of such faithfulness, possibilities that may continue unfolding long after we have been forgotten. To paraphrase Mordecai: who knows whether it is for such a time as this that we each have come to our particular place and moment?

? Questions for Reflection

1. Why is Ruth's non-Jewish status central to the understanding of this story?
2. What are some of the key themes in Ruth? Where in today's world do you see these themes at work?
3. What are some of the key themes in Esther? Where in today's world do you see these themes at work?
4. Compare the characters of Esther and Ruth. How were they similar? How were they different? How were the methods they used to achieve their goals similar? How were they different?

Bibliography

Esther

Beal, Timothy K. *Esther.* Berit Olam. Collegeville, Minn.: Liturgical Press, 1999.

Bechtel, Carol. *Esther.* Interpretation. Louisville, Ky.: John Knox Press, 2002.

Berlin, Adele. *Esther.* JPS Bible Commentary. Philadelphia: Jewish Publication Society, 2001.

Clines, David J. A. *The Esther Scroll: The Story of the Story.* JSOT Supplement Series. Sheffield: JSOT Press, 1984.

Crawford, Sidnie Ann White. "Esther." In *Women's Bible Commentary,* ed. Carol A. Newsom and Sharon H. Ringe. Louisville, Ky.: Westminster John Knox Press, 1998.

Crawford, Sidnie White. "Esther." In vol. 3, *The New Interpreter's Bible,* ed. Leander Keck. Nashville: Abingdon Press, 1999.

Day, Linda. *Three Faces of a Queen: Characterization in the Books of Esther.* Sheffield: Sheffield Academic Press, 1995.

Fox, Michael V. *Character and Ideology in the Book of Esther.* Studies in Biblical Personalities. Columbia, S.C.: University of South Carolina Press, 1991.

Levenson, Jon. *Esther: A Commentary.* Old Testament Library. Louisville, Ky.: Westminster John Knox Press, 1997.

Moore, Carey A. *Esther.* Anchor Bible. Garden City, N.Y.: Doubleday, 1971.

Tull, Patricia. *Esther's Feast: A Study of the Book of Esther.* Louisville, Ky.: Horizons, Presbyterian Women, PC(USA), 2001.

Van Wijk-Bos, Johanna W. H. *Ruth and Esther: Women in Alien Lands.* Nashville: Abingdon Press, 2001.

Ruth

Campbell, Edward F., Jr. *Ruth.* Anchor Bible. New York: Doubleday, 1975.

Farmer, Kathleen A. Robertson. "The Book of Ruth." In vol. 2, *The New Interpreter's Bible,* ed. Leander Keck. Nashville: Abingdon Press, 1998.

Fewell, Danna Nolan, and David Gunn. *Compromising Redemption: Relating Characters in the Book of Ruth.* Literary Currents in Biblical Interpretation. Louisville, Ky.: Westminster John Knox Press, 1990.

Levine, Amy-Jill. "Ruth." In *The Women's Bible Commentary*, ed. Carol A. Newsom and Sharon H. Ringe. Louisville, Ky.: Westminster John Knox Press, 1998.

Linafelt, Tod A. *Ruth*. Berit Olam. Collegeville, Minn.: Liturgical Press, 1999.

Nielsen, Kirsten. *Ruth*. Old Testament Library. Louisville, Ky.: Westminster John Knox Press, 1997.

Sakenfeld, Katharine Doob. *Ruth*. Interpretation. Louisville, Ky.: John Knox Press, 1999.

Trible, Phyllis. *God and the Rhetoric of Sexuality*. Philadelphia: Fortress Press, 1978.

Van Wijk-Bos, Johanna W. H. *Ruth and Esther: Women in Alien Lands*. Nashville: Abingdon Press, 2001.

Interpretation Bible Studies
Leader's Guide

Interpretation Bible Studies (IBS), for adults and older youth, are flexible, attractive, easy-to-use, and filled with solid information about the Bible. IBS helps Christians discover the guidance and power of the scriptures for living today. Perhaps you are leading a church school class, a mid-week Bible study group, or a youth group meeting, or simply using this in your own personal study. Whatever the setting may be, we hope you find this *Leader's Guide* helpful. Since every context and group is different, this *Leader's Guide* does not presume to tell you how to structure Bible study for your situation. Instead, the *Leader's Guide* seeks to offer choices—a number of helpful suggestions for leading a successful Bible study using IBS.

> "The church that no longer hears the essential message of the Scriptures soon ceases to understand what it is for and is open to be captured by the dominant religious philosophy of the moment."—James D. Smart, *The Strange Silence of the Bible in the Church: A Study in Hermeneutics* (Philadelphia: Westminster Press, 1970), 10.

How Should I Teach IBS?

1. Explore the Format

There is a wealth of information in IBS, perhaps more than you can use in one session. In this case, more is better. IBS has been designed to give you a well-stocked buffet of content and teachable insights. Pick and choose what suits your group's needs. Perhaps you will want to split units into two or more sessions, or combine units into a single session. Perhaps you will decide to use only a portion of a unit and then move on to the next unit. *There is not a structured theme or teaching focus to each unit that must be followed for IBS to be used.* Rather, IBS offers the flexibility to adjust to whatever suits your context.

A recent survey of both professional and volunteer church educators revealed that their number one concern was that Bible study materials be teacher-friendly. IBS is indeed teacher-friendly in two important ways. First, since IBS provides abundant content and a flexible design, teachers can shape the lessons creatively, responding to the needs of the group and employing a wide variety of teaching methods. Second, those who wish more specific suggestions for planning the sessions can find them at the Westminster John Knox Press Web site on the Internet (**www.ppcpub.org**). Click the "Free Downloads" button to access teaching suggestions for each IBS unit as well as helpful quotations, selections from Bible dictionaries and encyclopedias, and other teaching helps.

> "The more we bring to the Bible, the more we get from the Bible."—William Barclay, *A Beginner's Guide to the New Testament* (Louisville, Ky.: Westminster John Knox Press, 1995), vii.

IBS is not only teacher-friendly, it is also discussion-friendly. Given the opportunity, most adults and young people relish the chance to talk about the kind of issues raised in IBS. The secret, then, is to determine what works with your group, what will get them to talk. Several good methods for stimulating discussion are presented in this *Leader's Guide*, and once you learn your group, you can apply one of these methods and get the group discussing the Bible and its relevance in their lives.

The format of every IBS unit consists of several features:

a. Body of the Unit. This is the main content, consisting of interesting and informative commentary on the passage and scholarly insight into the biblical text and its significance for Christians today.

b. Sidebars. These are boxes that appear scattered throughout the body of the unit, with maps, photos, quotations, and intriguing ideas. Some sidebars can be identified quickly by a symbol, or icon, that helps the reader know what type of information can be found in that sidebar. There are icons for illustrations, key terms, pertinent quotes, and more.

c. Want to Know More? Each unit includes a "Want to Know More?" section that guides learners who wish to dig deeper and consult other resources. If your church library does not have the resources mentioned, you can look up the information in other standard Bible dictionaries, encyclopedias, and handbooks, or you can find much of this information at the Westminster John Knox Press Web site (see last page of this Guide).

d. Questions for Reflection. The unit ends with questions to help the learners think more deeply about the biblical passage and its pertinence for today. These questions are provided as examples only, and teachers are encouraged both to develop their own list of questions and to gather questions from the group. These discussion questions do not usually have specific "correct" answers. Again, the

> "The trick is to make the Bible our book."—Duncan S. Ferguson, *Bible Basics: Mastering the Content of the Bible* (Louisville, Ky.: Westminster John Knox Press, 1995), 3.

flexibility of IBS allows you to use these questions at the end of the group time, at the beginning, interspersed throughout, or not at all.

2. Select a Teaching Method

Here are ten suggestions. The format of IBS allows you to choose what direction you will take as you plan to teach. Only you will know how your lesson should best be designed for your group. Some adult groups prefer the lecture method, while others prefer a high level of free-ranging discussion. Many youth groups like interaction, activity, the use of music, and the chance to talk about their own experiences and feelings. Here is a list of a few possible approaches. Let your own creativity add to the list!

a. Let's Talk about What We've Learned. In this approach, all group members are requested to read the scripture passage and the IBS unit before the group meets. Ask the group members to make notes about the main issues, concerns, and questions they see in the passage. When the group meets, these notes are collected, shared, and discussed. This method depends, of course, on the group's willingness to do some "homework."

b. What Do We Want and Need to Know? This approach begins by having the whole group read the scripture passage together. Then, drawing from your study of the IBS, you, as the teacher, write on a board or flip chart two lists:

(1) Things we should know to better understand this passage (content information related to the passage, for example, historical insights about political contexts, geographical landmarks, economic nuances, etc.), and

> "Although small groups can meet for many purposes and draw upon many different resources, the one resource which has shaped the life of the Church more than any other throughout its long history has been the Bible."—Roberta Hestenes, *Using the Bible in Groups* (Philadelphia: Westminster Press, 1983), 14.

(2) Four or five "important issues we should talk about regarding this passage" (with implications for today—how the issues in the biblical context continue into today, for example, issues of idolatry or fear).

Allow the group to add to either list, if they wish, and use the lists to lead into a time of learning, reflection, and discussion. This approach is suitable for those settings where there is little or no advanced preparation by the students.

c. Hunting and Gathering. Start the unit by having the group read the scripture passage together. Then divide the group into smaller clusters (perhaps having as few as one person), each with a different assignment. Some clusters can discuss one or more of the "Questions for Reflection." Others can look up key terms or people in a Bible dictionary or track down other biblical references found in the body of the unit. After the small clusters have had time to complete their tasks, gather the entire group again and lead them through the study material, allowing each cluster to contribute what it learned.

d. From Question Mark to Exclamation Point. This approach begins with contemporary questions and then moves to the biblical content as a response to those questions. One way to do this is for you to ask the group, at the beginning of the class, a rephrased version of one or more of the "Questions for Reflection" at the end of the study unit. For example, one of the questions at the end of the unit on Exodus 3:1–4:17 in the IBS *Exodus* volume reads,

> Moses raised four protests, or objections, to God's call. Contemporary people also raise objections to God's call. In what ways are these similar to Moses' protests? In what ways are they different?

This question assumes familiarity with the biblical passage about Moses, so the question would not work well before the group has explored the passage. However, try rephrasing this question as an opening exercise; for example:

Here is a thought experiment: Let's assume that God, who called people in the Bible to do daring and risky things, still calls people today to tasks of faith and courage. In the Bible, God called Moses from a burning bush and called Isaiah in a moment of ecstatic worship in the Temple. How do you think God's call is experienced by people today? Where do you see evidence of people saying "yes" to God's call? When people say "no" or raise an objection to God's call, what reasons do they give (to themselves, to God)?

Posing this or a similar question at the beginning will generate discussion and raise important issues, and then it can lead the group into an exploration of the biblical passage as a resource for thinking even more deeply about these questions.

e. Let's Go to the Library. From your church library, your pastor's library, or other sources, gather several good commentaries on the book of the Bible you are studying. Among the trustworthy commentaries are those in the Interpretation studies (John Knox Press) and the Westminster Bible Companion series (Westminster John Knox Press). Divide your groups into smaller clusters and give one commentary to each cluster (one or more of the clusters can be given the IBS volume instead of a full-length commentary). Ask each cluster to read the biblical passage you are studying and then to read the section of the commentary that covers that passage (if your group is large, you may want to make photocopies of the commentary material with proper permission, of course). The task of each cluster is to name the two or three most important insights they discover about the biblical passage by reading and talking together about the commentary material. When you reassemble the larger group to share these insights, your group will gain not only a variety of insights about the passage but also a sense that differing views of the same text are par for the course in biblical interpretation.

f. Working Creatively Together. Begin with a creative group task, tied to the main thrust of the study. For example, if the study is on the Ten Commandments, a parable, or a psalm, have the group rewrite the Ten Commandments, the parable, or the psalm in contemporary language. If the passage is an epistle, have the group write a letter to their own congregation. Or if the study is a narrative, have the group role-play the characters in the story or write a page describing the story from the point of view of one of the characters. After completion of the task, read and discuss the biblical passage, asking for interpretations and applications from the group and tying in IBS material as it fits the flow of the discussion.

g. Singing Our Faith. Begin the session by singing (or reading) together a hymn that alludes to the biblical passage being studied (or to the theological themes in the passage). For example, if you are studying the unit from the IBS volume on Psalm 121, you can sing "I to the Hills Will Lift My Eyes," "Sing Praise to God, Who Reigns Above," or another hymn based on Psalm 121. Let the group reflect on the thoughts and feelings evoked by the hymn, then move to the biblical passage, allowing the biblical text and the IBS material to underscore, clarify, refine, and deepen the discussion stimulated by the hymn. If you are ambitious, you may ask the group to write a new hymn at the end of the study! (Many hymnals have indexes in the back or companion volumes that help the user match hymns to scripture passages or topics.)

h. Fill in the Blanks. In order to help the learners focus on the content of the biblical passage, at the beginning of the session ask each member of the group to read the biblical passage and fill out a brief questionnaire about the details of the passage (provide a copy for each learner or write the questions on the board). For example, if you are studying the unit in the IBS *Matthew* volume on Matthew 22:1–14, the questionnaire could include questions such as the following:

— In this story, Jesus compares the kingdom of heaven to what?
— List the various responses of those who were invited to the king's banquet but who did not come.
— When his invitation was rejected, how did the king feel? What did the king do?
— In the second part of the story, when the king saw a man at the banquet without a wedding garment, what did the king say? What did the man say? What did the king do?
— What is the saying found at the end of this story?

Gather the group's responses to the questions and perhaps encourage discussion. Then lead the group through the IBS material helping the learners to understand the meanings of these details and the significance of the passage for today. Feeling creative? Instead of a fill-in-the-blanks questionnaire, create a crossword puzzle from names and words in the biblical passage.

i. Get the Picture. In this approach, stimulate group discussion by incorporating a painting, photograph, or other visual object into the lesson. You can begin by having the group examine and comment on this visual or you can introduce the visual later in the lesson—it depends on the object used. If, for example, you are studying the unit Exodus 3:1–4:17 in the IBS *Exodus* volume, you may want to view Paul Koli's very colorful painting *The Burning Bush*. Two sources for this painting are *The Bible through Asian Eyes,* edited by Masao Takenaka and Ron O'Grady (National City, Calif.: Pace Publishing Co., 1991), and *Imaging the Word: An Arts and Lectionary Resource,* vol. 3, edited by Susan A. Blain (Cleveland: United Church Press, 1996).

j. Now Hear This. Especially if your class is large, you may want to use the lecture method. As the teacher, you prepare a presentation on the biblical passage, using as many resources as you have available plus your own experience, but following the content of the IBS unit as a guide. You can make the lecture even more lively by asking the learners at various points along the way to refer to the visuals and quotes found in the "sidebars." A place can be made for questions (like the ones at the end of the unit)—either at the close of the lecture or at strategic points along the way.

> "It is . . . important to call a Bible study group back to what the text being discussed actually says, especially when an individual has gotten off on some tangent."—Richard Robert Osmer, *Teaching for Faith: A Guide for Teachers of Adult Classes* (Louisville, Ky.: Westminster John Knox Press, 1992), 71.

3. Keep These Teaching Tips in Mind

There are no surefire guarantees for a teaching success. However, the following suggestions can increase the chances for a successful study:

a. Always Know Where the Group Is Headed. Take ample time beforehand to prepare the material. Know the main points of the study, and know the destination. Be flexible, and encourage discussion, but don't lose sight of where you are headed.

b. Ask Good Questions; Don't Be Afraid of Silence. Ideally, a discussion blossoms spontaneously from the reading of the scripture. But more often than not, a discussion must be drawn from the group members by a series of well-chosen questions. After asking each question, give the group members time to answer. Let them think, and don't be threatened by a season of silence. Don't feel that every question must have an answer, and that as leader, you must supply every answer. Facilitate discussion by getting the group members to cooperate with each other. Sometimes the original question can be restated. Sometimes it is helpful to ask a follow-up question like "What makes this a hard question to answer?"

Ask questions that encourage explanatory answers. Try to avoid questions that can be answered simply "Yes" or "No." Rather than asking, "Do you think Moses was frightened by the burning bush?" ask, "What do you think Moses was feeling and experiencing as he stood before the burning bush?" If group members answer with just one word, ask a follow-up question like "Why do you think this is so?" Ask questions about their feelings and opinions, mixed within questions about facts or details. Repeat their responses or restate their response to reinforce their contributions to the group.

> "Studies of learning reveal that while people remember approximately 10% of what they hear, they remember up to 90% of what they say. Therefore, to increase the amount of learning that occurs, increase the amount of talking about the Bible which each member does."—Roberta Hestenes, *Using the Bible in Groups* (Philadelphia: Westminster Press, 1983), 17.

Most studies can generate discussion by asking open-ended questions. Depending on the group, several types of questions can work. Some groups will respond well to content questions that can be answered from reading the IBS comments or the biblical passage. Others will respond well to questions about feelings or thoughts. Still others will respond to questions that challenge them to new thoughts or that may not have exact answers. Be sensitive to the group's dynamic in choosing questions.

Some suggested questions are: What is the point of the passage? Who are the main characters? Where is the tension in the story? Why does it say (this) _____, and not (that) _____? What raises questions for you? What terms need defining? What are the new ideas? What doesn't make sense? What bothers or troubles you about this passage? What keeps you from living the truth of this passage?

c. Don't Settle for the Ordinary. There is nothing like a surprise. Think of special or unique ways to present the ideas of the study. Upset the applecart of the ordinary. Even though the passage may be familiar, look for ways to introduce suspense. Remember that a little mystery can capture the imagination. Change your routine.

Along with the element of surprise, humor can open up a discussion. Don't be afraid to laugh. A well-chosen joke or cartoon may present the central theme in a way that a lecture would have stymied.

Sometimes a passage is too familiar. No one speaks up because everyone feels that all that could be said has been said. Choose an unfamiliar translation from which to read, or if the passage is from a Gospel, compare the story across two or more Gospels and note differences. It is amazing what insights can be drawn from seeing something strange in what was thought to be familiar.

d. Feel Free to Supplement the IBS Resources with Other Material. Consult other commentaries to resources. Tie in current events with the lesson. Scour newspapers or magazines for stories that touch on the issues of the study. Sometimes the lyrics of a song, or a section of prose from a well-written novel, will be just the right seasoning for the study.

e. And Don't Forget to Check the Web. Check out our site on the World Wide Web (**www.ppcpub.org**). Click the "Free Downloads" button to access teaching suggestions. Several possibilities for applying the teaching methods suggested above for individual IBS units will be available. Feel free to download this material.

f. Stay Close to the Biblical Text. Don't forget that the goal is to learn the Bible. Return to the text again and again. Avoid making the mistake of reading the passage only at the beginning of the study, and then wandering away to comments on top of comments from that point on. Trust in the power and presence of the Holy Spirit to use the truths of the passage to work within the lives of the study participants.

> "The Bible is literature, but it is much more than literature. It is the holy book of Jews and Christians, who find there a manifestation of God's presence."—Kathleen Norris, *The Psalms* (New York: Riverhead Books, 1997), xxii.

What If Am Using IBS in Personal Bible Study?

If you are using IBS in your personal Bible study, you can experiment and explore a variety of ways. You may choose to read straight through the study without giving any attention to the sidebars or other features. Or you may find yourself interested in a question or unfamiliar with a key term, and you can allow the sidebars "Want to Know More?" and "Questions for Reflection" to lead you into deeper learning on these issues. Perhaps you will want to have a few commentaries or a Bible dictionary available to pursue what interests you. As was suggested in one of the teaching methods above, you may want to begin with the questions at the end, and then read the Bible passage followed by the IBS material. Trust the IBS resources to provide good and helpful information, and then follow your interests!

Want to Know More?

About leading Bible study groups? See Roberta Hestenes, *Using the Bible in Groups* (Philadelphia: Westminster Press, 1983).

About basic Bible content? See Duncan S. Ferguson, *Bible Basics: Mastering the Content of the Bible* (Louisville, Ky.: Westminster John Knox Press, 1995); William M. Ramsay, *The Westminster Guide to the Books of the Bible* (Louisville, Ky.: Westminster John Knox Press, 1994).

About the development of the Bible? See John Barton, *How the Bible Came to Be* (Louisville, Ky.: Westminster John Knox Press, 1997).

About the meaning of difficult terms? See Donald K. McKim, *Westminster Dictionary of Theological Terms* (Louisville, Ky.: Westminster John Knox Press, 1996); Paul J. Achtemeier, *Harper's Bible Dictionary* (San Francisco: Harper & Row, 1985).

For more information about IBS,

click the "Free Downloads" button at

www.ppcpub.org